30
Essential
Lessons
from
Women
of the Bible

Freeman-Smith, a division of Worthy Media, Inc.
134 Franklin Road, Suite 200, Brentwood, Tennessee 37027

The quoted ideas expressed in this book (but not Scripture verses) are not, in all cases, exact quotations, as some have been edited for clarity and brevity. In all cases, the author has attempted to maintain the speaker's original intent. In some cases, quoted material for this book was obtained from secondary sources, primarily print media. While every effort was made to ensure the accuracy of these sources, the accuracy cannot be guaranteed. For additions, deletions, corrections, or clarifications in future editions of this text, please write Freeman-Smith.

Scripture quotations are taken from:

The Holy Bible, King James Version

The Holy Bible, New International Version (NIV) Copyright © 1973, 1978, 1984, by International Bible Society. Used by permission of Zondervan Publishing House. All rights reserved.

The Holy Bible, New King James Version (NKJV) Copyright © 1982 by Thomas Nelson, Inc. Used by permission.

The Holy Bible, New Living Translation, (NLT) Copyright © 1996. Used by permission of Tyndale House Publishers, Inc., Wheaton, Illinois 60189. All rights reserved.

The New American Standard Bible®, (NASB) Copyright © 1960, 1962, 1963, 1968, 1971, 1972, 1973, 1975, 1977, 1995 by The Lockman Foundation. Used by permission.

The Message (MSG)- This edition issued by contractual arrangement with NavPress, a division of The Navigators, U.S.A. Originally published by NavPress in English as THE MESSAGE: The Bible in Contemporary Language copyright 2002-2003 by Eugene Peterson. All rights reserved.

The Holman Christian Standard Bible™ (HCSB) Copyright © 1999, 2000, 2001 by Holman Bible Publishers. Used by permission.

Cover Design by Kim Russell / Wahoo Designs
Page Layout by Bart Dawson

ISBN 978-1-60587-343-5

30 Essential Lessons from Women of the Bible

Table of Contents

Introduction

We have much to learn from women of the Bible, and this book is intended to help by sharing 30 essential lessons from the lives of Mary, Eve, Sarah, Deborah, Ruth, Esther, Lydia, Mary Magdalene, two unnamed women, and the two sisters of Lazarus: Mary and Martha.

The fabric of daily life is woven together with the threads of habit, and no habit is more important than that of consistent prayer and daily devotion to the Creator. God's Word is not a distant document designed only for the people of ancient times; it is a living document intended for you.

So, during the next 30 days, please try this experiment: read a chapter from this book each day and try to find at least one essential lesson that you can employ immediately. If you're already committed to a daily time of worship, this book will enrich that experience. If you are not, the simple act of giving God a few minutes each morning will change the direction of your day and the quality of your life.

Mary, the Mother of Jesus

Relatively little is known of her personal history, but the most important aspects of her life story are familiar to Christians—and to non-Christians—the world over. She was Mary of Nazareth, the blessed virgin, the mother of our Lord, Jesus Christ.

In the Gospel According to Luke, we learn that Mary was chosen by God to bear His Son:

Now in the sixth month the angel Gabriel was sent by God to a city of Galilee named Nazareth, to a virgin betrothed to a man whose name was Joseph, of the house of David.

The virgin's name was Mary. And having come in, the angel said to her, "Rejoice, highly favored one, the Lord is with you; blessed are you among women!" But when she saw him, she was troubled at his saying, and considered what manner of greeting this was. Then the angel said to her, "Do not be afraid, Mary, for you have found favor with God. And behold, you will conceive in your womb and bring forth a Son, and shall call His name Jesus. He will be great, and will be called the Son of the Highest; and the Lord God will give Him the throne of His father David. And He will reign over the house of Jacob forever, and of His kingdom there will be no end."

Then Mary said to the angel, "How can this be, since I do not know a man?" And the angel answered and said to her, "The Holy Spirit will come upon you, and the power of the Highest will overshadow you; therefore, also, that Holy One who is to be born will be called the Son of God. Now indeed, Elizabeth your relative has also conceived a son in her old age; and this is now the sixth month for her who was called barren. For with God nothing will be impossible." Then Mary said, "Behold the maidservant of the Lord! Let it be to me according to your word." And the angel departed from her.

Luke 1:26-38 NKJV

There can be no doubt that Mary was chosen among women, blessed by God to be the recipient of divine guidance and grace. She was chosen by the Creator to bear His Son, and when God's angel announced His intentions to her, Mary believed.

In the first three chapters of this text, we will examine Mary's faith and the essential lessons we can glean from her life.

Lesson 1

God Can Do Anything

Ah, Lord God! Behold, You have made the heavens and the earth by Your great power and outstretched arm. There is nothing too hard for You.

Jeremiah 32:17 NKJV

THE LESSON

Mary discovered that God works in miraculous ways. And you can discover that fact, too, if you keep your eyes and your heart open.

Mary, who lived in Nazareth, was engaged to a carpenter named Joseph. But before the two were married, an angel appeared to Mary and revealed miraculous news: she would become pregnant with God's Son by the Holy Spirit.

God is a miracle worker. Throughout history, He has intervened in the course of human events in ways that cannot be explained by science or human rationale. And He's still doing so today.

God's miracles are not limited to special occasions, nor are they witnessed by a select few. God is crafting His wonders all around us: the miracle of the birth of a new baby; the miracle of a world renewing itself with every sunrise; the miracle of lives transformed by God's love and grace. Each day, God's handiwork is evident for all to see and experience.

Today, seize the opportunity to inspect God's hand at work. His miracles come in a variety of shapes and sizes, so keep your eyes and your heart open. Be watchful, and you'll soon be amazed.

SOMETHING TO THINK ABOUT

God has infinite power. If you're watchful, you'll observe many miracles. So keep your eyes, your heart, and your mind open.

When we face an impossible situation, all self-reliance and self-confidence must melt away; we must be totally dependent on Him for the resources.

Anne Graham Lotz

There is Someone who makes possible what seems completely impossible.

Catherine Marshall

Only God can move mountains, but faith and prayer can move God.

E. M. Bounds

Miracles broke the physical laws of the universe; forgiveness broke the moral rules.

Philip Yancey

The impossible is exactly what God does.

Oswald Chambers

Are you looking for a miracle? If you keep your eyes wide open and trust in God, you won't have to look very far.

Marie T. Freeman

I could go through this day oblivious to the miracles all around me or I could tune in and "enjoy."

Gloria Gaither

Faith means believing in realities that go beyond sense and sight. It is the awareness of unseen divine realities all around you.

Joni Eareckson Tada

Prayer succeeds when all else fails.

E. M. Bounds

The miracles in fact are a retelling in small letters of the very same story which is written across the whole world in letters too large for some of us to see.

C. S. Lewis

MORE FROM GOD'S WORD

Looking at them, Jesus said, "With men it is impossible, but not with God, because all things are possible with God."

Mark 10:27 HCSB

But as it is written: "Eye has not seen, nor ear heard, nor have entered into the heart of man the things which God has prepared for those who love Him."

1 Corinthians 2:9 NKJV

I assure you: The one who believes in Me will also do the works that I do. And he will do even greater works than these, because I am going to the Father.

John 14:12 HCSB

You are the God who works wonders; You revealed Your strength among the peoples.

Psalm 77:14 HCSB

For nothing will be impossible with God.

Luke 1:37 HCSB

MY THOUGHTS ON THIS LESSON

_____

_____

_____

_____

_____

_____

_____

_____

_____

_____

A PRAYER FOR TODAY

Dear God, Mary's life, and the birth of Your Son, remind me
that nothing is impossible for You. Your infinite power is beyond
human understanding—keep me always mindful of Your strength.
When I lose hope, give me faith; when others lose hope,
let me tell them of Your glory and Your works. Today, Lord,
let me expect the miraculous, and let me trust in You. Amen

When We Trust God Completely, Great Things Happen

So it was, when the angels had gone away from them into heaven, that the shepherds said to one another, "Let us now go to Bethlehem and see this thing that has come to pass, which the Lord has made known to us." And they came with haste and found Mary and Joseph, and the Babe lying in a manger. Now when they had seen Him, they made widely known the saying which was told them concerning this Child. And all those who heard it marveled at those things which were told them by the shepherds. But Mary kept all these things and pondered them in her heart.

Luke 2:15-19 NKJV

THE LESSON

When Mary trusted God, He used her in a wonderful way. And, when you trust God, He will use you in a wonderful way, too.

Mary trusted God and followed His instructions to the letter. Of course, Mary's trust was rewarded. And when we trust God completely and without reservation, we're rewarded, too.

It's easy to talk about trusting God, but when it comes to actually trusting Him, that's considerably harder. Why? Because genuine trust in God requires more than words; it requires a willingness to follow God's lead and a willingness to obey His commandments.

Have you spent more time talking about Christ than walking in His footsteps? If so, God wants to have a little chat with you. And, if you're unwilling to talk to Him, He may take other actions in order to grab your attention.

Thankfully, whenever you're willing to talk with God, He's willing to listen. And, the instant that you decide to place Him squarely in the center of your life, He will respond to that decision with blessings that are too unexpected to predict and too numerous to count.

> When God blesses us, He expects us to use those blessings to bless the lives of others.
>
> —
>
> *Jim Gallery*

The next time you find your courage tested to the limit, lean upon God's promises. Trust His Son. Remember that God is always near and that He is your protector and your deliverer. When you are worried, anxious, or afraid, call upon Him. God can handle your troubles infinitely better than you can, so turn them over to Him. Remember that God rules both mountaintops and valleys—with limitless wisdom and love—now and forever.

> ## Something to Think about
>
> Because God is trustworthy—and because He has made promises to you that He intends to keep—you are protected.

Sometimes the very essence of faith is trusting God in the midst of things He knows good and well we cannot comprehend.

Beth Moore

A prayerful heart and an obedient heart will learn, very slowly and not without sorrow, to stake everything on God Himself.

Elisabeth Elliot

Trusting in my own mental understanding becomes a hindrance to complete trust in God.

Oswald Chambers

Never be afraid to trust an unknown future to a known God.

Corrie ten Boom

Are you serious about wanting God's guidance to become the person he wants you to be? The first step is to tell God that you know you can't manage your own life; that you need his help.

Catherine Marshall

Because God is my sovereign Lord, I was not worried. He manages perfectly, day and night, year in and year out, the movements of the stars, the wheeling of the planets, the staggering coordination of events that goes on at the molecular level in order to hold things together. There is no doubt that he can manage the timing of my days and weeks.

Elisabeth Elliot

We prevent God from giving us the great spiritual gifts He has in store for us, because we do not give thanks for daily gifts.

Dietrich Bonhoeffer

Grace comes from the heart of a gracious God who wants to stun you and overwhelm you with a gift you don't deserve—salvation, adoption, a spiritual ability to use in kingdom service, answered prayer, the church, His presence, His wisdom, His guidance, His love.

Bill Hybels

MORE FROM GOD'S WORD

For the eyes of the Lord range throughout the earth to show Himself strong for those whose hearts are completely His.

2 Chronicles 16:9 HCSB

He granted their request because they trusted in Him.

1 Chronicles 5:20 HCSB

Let us hold fast the confession of our hope without wavering, for He who promised is faithful.

Hebrews 10:23 NKJV

The one who understands a matter finds success, and the one who trusts in the Lord will be happy.

Proverbs 16:20 HCSB

For we walk by faith, not by sight.

2 Corinthians 5:7 NKJV

MY THOUGHTS ON THIS LESSON

_____

_____

_____

_____

_____

_____

_____

_____

_____

_____

A PRAYER FOR TODAY

Today, Lord, I will trust You and seek Your will for my life.
You have a plan for me, Father. Let me discover it and live it,
knowing that when I trust in You, I am eternally blessed. Amen

Lesson 3

Purpose, According to God

Mary responded, "I am the Lord's servant.
May everything you have said about me come true."
And then the angel left her.

Luke 1:38 NLT

THE LESSON

God had a unique purpose for Mary, and He has a unique purpose for you.

When God made His plans clear to her, Mary did not resist nor did she complain. Instead, she accepted God's plan for her, and she followed His direction.

God had a perfect plan for Mary. And make no mistake: God also has a perfect plan for you, too. Your challenge is to discover that plan and, to the best of your ability, to follow it.

Life is best lived on purpose, not by accident: the sooner we discover what God intends for us to do with our lives, the better. But God's purposes aren't always clear to us. Sometimes we wander aimlessly in a wilderness of our own making. And sometimes, we struggle mightily against God in a vain effort to find success and happiness through our own means, not His.

> A person with no devotional life generally struggles with faith and obedience.
>
> —
>
> *Charles Stanley*

Whenever we struggle against God's plans, we suffer. When we resist God's calling, our efforts bear little fruit. Our best strategy, therefore, is to seek God's wisdom and to follow Him wherever He chooses to lead. When we do so, we are blessed.

When we align ourselves with God's purposes, we avail ourselves of His power and His peace. But how can we know precisely what God's intentions are? The answer, of course, is that even the most well-intentioned believers face periods of uncertainty and doubt about the direction of their lives. So, too, will you.

When you arrive at one of life's inevitable crossroads, that is precisely the moment when you should turn your thoughts and prayers toward God. When you do, He will make Himself known to you in a time and manner of His choosing.

Are you earnestly seeking to discern God's purpose for your life? If so, remember this: 1. God has a plan for your life; 2. If you seek that plan sincerely and prayerfully, you will find it; 3. When you discover God's purpose for your life, you will experience abundance, peace, joy, and power—God's power. And that's the only kind of power that really matters.

SOMETHING TO THINK ABOUT

When you gain a clear vision of your purpose for life here on earth—and for life everlasting—your steps will be sure.

His life is our light—our purpose and meaning and reason for living.

Anne Graham Lotz

Yesterday is just experience but tomorrow is glistening with purpose—and today is the channel leading from one to the other.

Barbara Johnson

Only God's chosen task for you will ultimately satisfy. Do not wait until it is too late to realize the privilege of serving Him in His chosen position for you.

Beth Moore

Aim at Heaven and you will get earth "thrown in"; aim at earth and you will get neither.

C. S. Lewis

God custom-designed you with your unique combination of personality, temperament, talents, and background, and He wants to harness and use these in His mission to reach this messed-up world.

Bill Hybels

MORE FROM GOD'S WORD

For it is God who is working among you both the willing and the working for His good purpose.

Philippians 2:13 HCSB

We know that all things work together for the good of those who love God: those who are called according to His purpose.

Romans 8:28 HCSB

I will instruct you and show you the way to go; with My eye on you, I will give counsel.

Psalm 32:8 HCSB

You reveal the path of life to me; in Your presence is abundant joy; in Your right hand are eternal pleasures.

Psalm 16:11 HCSB

Commit your activities to the Lord and your plans will be achieved.

Proverbs 16:3 HCSB

My Thoughts on This Lesson

_____

_____

_____

_____

_____

_____

_____

_____

_____

_____

A Prayer for Today

Dear Lord, You are the Creator of the universe, and I know
that Your plan for my life is grander than I can imagine.
Let Your purposes be my purposes, and let me trust in
the assurance of Your promises. Amen

Eve

Every schoolchild knows the name of Eve, the first woman, the wife of Adam, the mother of Cain and Abel, and the victim of the serpent's wiles. The familiar story of Eve's creation is told in Genesis:

And the Lord God said, "It is not good that man should be alone; I will make him a helper comparable to him." Out of the ground the Lord God formed every beast of the field and every bird of the air, and brought them to Adam to see what he would call them. And whatever Adam called each living creature, that was its name. So Adam gave names to all cattle, to the birds of the air, and to every beast of the field. But for Adam there was not found a helper comparable to him.

And the Lord God caused a deep sleep to fall on Adam, and he slept; and He took one of his ribs, and closed up the flesh in its place. Then the rib which the Lord God had taken from man He made into a woman, and He brought her to the man.

And Adam said:"This is now bone of my bones and flesh of my flesh; she shall be called Woman, because she was taken out of Man."

Therefore a man shall leave his father and mother and be joined to his wife, and they shall become one flesh.

Genesis 2:18-24 NKJV

Adam and Eve inhabited a glorious garden, a place of great beauty, a place without shame or want. But Eve was tempted by the serpent, and she succumbed to the serpent's lies. She disobeyed God, ate the forbidden fruit, induced her husband to do the same, and became a cautionary example for those who are foolish enough to defy the instructions of the Creator.

Lesson 4

Satan Is Near

And the Lord God said to the woman,
"What is this you have done?" The woman said,
"The serpent deceived me, and I ate."

Genesis 3:13 NKJV

THE LESSON

As Eve discovered, Satan is deceptive, dangerous, persistent, patient, and near.

This world is God's creation, and it contains the wonderful fruits of His handiwork. But, the world also contains countless opportunities to stray from God's will. But as Eve discovered, temptations are never very far away, and Satan, it seems, never takes a day off. Our task, as believers, is to turn away from temptation and to place our lives squarely in the center of God's will.

What was true in the Garden of Eden is equally true in our own. Evil is indeed abroad in the world, and Satan continues to sow the seeds of destruction far and wide. In a very real sense, our world is at war: good versus evil, sin versus righteousness, hope versus suffering, praise versus apathy. As Christians, we must ensure that we place ourselves squarely on the right side of these conflicts: God's side. How can we do it? By thoughtfully studying God's Word, by regularly worshiping with fellow believers, and by guarding our hearts and minds against the subtle temptations of the enemy. When we do, we are protected.

> Flee temptation
> without leaving
> a forwarding address.
>
> —
>
> *Barbara Johnson*

Are you determined to stand up against evil whenever and wherever you confront it? And are you fully prepared to distance yourself from the countless temptations that have become so thoroughly woven into the fabric of society? If so, congratulations. That means you're an active-duty participant in the battle against a powerful and dangerous adversary. And with God's help, you're destined to win the battle and the war.

SOMETHING TO THINK ABOUT

Evil exists, and it exists someplace not too far from you. You must guard your steps and your heart accordingly.

It is easier to stay out of temptation than to get out of it.

Rick Warren

There is sharp necessity for giving Christ absolute obedience. The devil bids for our complete self-will. To whatever extent we give this self-will the right to be master over our lives, we are, to an extent, giving Satan a toehold.

Catherine Marshall

Deception is the enemy's ongoing plan of attack.

Stormie Omartian

Lord, what joy to know that Your powers are so much greater than those of the enemy.

Corrie ten Boom

The Bible teaches us in times of temptation there is one command: Flee! Get away from it, for every struggle against lust using only one's own strength is doomed to failure.

Dietrich Bonhoeffer

Instant intimacy is one of the leading warning signals of a seduction.

Beth Moore

Many times the greatest temptations confront us when we are in the center of the will of God, because being there has offset and frustrated Satans' methods of attack.

Franklin Graham

Temptation is not a sin. Even Jesus was tempted. The Lord Jesus gives you the strength needed to resist temptation.

Corrie ten Boom

The Scriptures were not given for our information, but for our transformation.

D. L. Moody

MORE FROM GOD'S WORD

No temptation has overtaken you except what is common to humanity. God is faithful and He will not allow you to be tempted beyond what you are able, but with the temptation He will also provide a way of escape, so that you are able to bear it.

1 Corinthians 10:13 HCSB

For we do not have a High Priest who cannot sympathize with our weaknesses, but was in all points tempted as we are, yet without sin. Let us therefore come boldly to the throne of grace, that we may obtain mercy and find grace to help in time of need.

Hebrews 4:15-16 NKJV

Put on the whole armor of God, that you may be able to stand against the wiles of the devil.

Ephesians 6:11 NKJV

Be sober! Be on the alert! Your adversary the Devil is prowling around like a roaring lion, looking for anyone he can devour.

1 Peter 5:8 HCSB

The Lord knows how to deliver the godly out of temptations.

2 Peter 2:9 NKJV

MY THOUGHTS ON THIS LESSON

_____

_____

_____

_____

_____

_____

_____

_____

_____

_____

A PRAYER FOR TODAY

Lord, strengthen my walk with You. Evil comes in many disguises,
and sometimes it is only with Your help that I can recognize right
from wrong. Your presence in my life enables me to choose truth
and to live a life pleasing to You. May I always live
in Your presence. Amen

Sarah

S arah was a beautiful woman, the devoted wife of Abraham, and the mother of Isaac, a child she bore when she was 90 years old. Sarah's life stands as a powerful example of this essential fact: God always keeps His promises.

In the following passage, we learn of God's pledge to Abraham, a pledge that seemed impossible to Abraham:

> Then God said to Abraham, "As for Sarai your wife, you shall not call her name Sarai, but Sarah shall be her name. And I will bless her and also give you a son by her; then I will bless her, and she shall be a mother of nations; kings of peoples shall be from her."
>
> Then Abraham fell on his face and laughed, and said in his heart, "Shall a child be born to a man who is one hundred years old? And shall Sarah, who is ninety years old, bear a child?" And Abraham said to God, "Oh, that Ishmael might live before You!"
>
> Then God said: "No, Sarah your wife shall bear you a son, and you shall call his name Isaac; I will establish My covenant with him for an everlasting covenant, and with his descendants after him. And as for Ishmael, I have heard you. Behold, I have blessed him, and will make him fruitful, and will multiply him exceedingly. He shall beget twelve princes, and I will make him a great nation. But My covenant I

will establish with Isaac, whom Sarah shall bear to you at this set time next year." Then He finished talking with him, and God went up from Abraham.

Genesis 17:15-22 NKJV

As you read the following chapter, please remember that just as God kept His promise to Abraham and Sarah, so, too, will He keep His promises to you.

Lesson 5

God Keeps His Promises

Then Abraham bowed down to the ground, but he laughed to himself in disbelief. "How could I become a father at the age of 100?" he thought. "And how can Sarah have a baby when she is ninety years old?" So Abraham said to God, "May Ishmael live under your special blessing!" But God replied, "No—Sarah, your wife, will give birth to a son for you. You will name him Isaac, and I will confirm my covenant with him and his descendants as an everlasting covenant."

Genesis 17:17-19 NLT

THE LESSON

When God makes a covenant, He keeps it. And, because God is trustworthy, you can have faith.

God made a promise to Abraham, a promise that Sarah would bear him a son. But, to Abraham, God's promise seemed improbable at best and impossible at worst. But God fulfilled His promise—as He always does—so Sarah gave birth to Isaac.

God has made quite a few promises to you, and He will keep every single one of them. Elisabeth Elliot observed, "We have ample evidence that the Lord is able to guide. The promises cover every imaginable situation. All we need to do is to take the hand he stretches out." And her words apply to you and to every situation you will ever encounter.

Are you facing a difficult decision? Pause for a moment and have a quiet consultation with your ultimate Advisor. Are you fearful, anxious, fretful, or troubled? Slow yourself down long enough to consider God's promises. Those promises never fail and they never grow old. You can trust those promises, and you can share them with your family, with your friends, and with the world . . . starting now . . . and ending never.

> Either God's Word keeps you from sin, or sin keeps you from God's Word.
>
> —
>
> *Corrie ten Boom*

SOMETHING TO THINK ABOUT

Today, think about the role that God's Word plays in your life, and think about ways that you can worry less and trust God more.

It takes calm, thoughtful, prayerful meditation on the Word to extract its deepest nourishment.

Vance Havner

The Bible is God's Word to man.

Kay Arthur

Help me, Lord, to be a student of Your Word, that I might be a better servant in Your world.

Jim Gallery

Walk in the daylight of God's will because then you will be safe; you will not stumble.

Anne Graham Lotz

Weave the unveiling fabric of God's word through your heart and mind. It will hold strong, even if the rest of life unravels.

Gigi Graham Tchividjian

My meditation and study have shown me that, like God, His Word is holy, everlasting, absolutely true, powerful, personally fair, and never changing.

Bill Bright

Words fail to express my love for this holy Book, my gratitude for its author, for His love and goodness. How shall I thank him for it?

Lottie Moon

The Holy Spirit is the Spirit of Truth, which means He always works according to and through the Word of God whether you feel Him or not.

Anne Graham Lotz

The remarkable thing about fearing God is that when you fear God, you fear nothing else, whereas if you do not fear God, you fear everything else.

Oswald Chambers

MORE FROM GOD'S WORD

Heaven and earth will pass away, but My words will never pass away.

Matthew 24:35 HCSB

But the word of the Lord endures forever. And this is the word that was preached as the gospel to you.

1 Peter 1:25 HCSB

All Scripture is inspired by God and is profitable for teaching, for rebuking, for correcting, for training in righteousness, so that the man of God may be complete, equipped for every good work.

2 Timothy 3:16-17 HCSB

For the word of God is living and effective and sharper than any two-edged sword, penetrating as far as to divide soul, spirit, joints, and marrow; it is a judge of the ideas and thoughts of the heart.

Hebrews 4:12 HCSB

The one who is from God listens to God's words. This is why you don't listen, because you are not from God.

John 8:47 HCSB

MY THOUGHTS ON THIS LESSON

_____

_____

_____

_____

_____

_____

_____

_____

_____

_____

A PRAYER FOR TODAY

Lord, Your Holy Word contains promises, and I will trust them.
I will use the Bible as my guide, and I will trust You, Lord,
to speak to me through Your Holy Spirit and through
Your Holy Word, this day and forever. Amen

Deborah

Deborah was a strong woman, a judge, a military leader of the Israelites, and a prophetess. The following passage describes how she instructed Barak who, in turn, led the people of Israel in victory over the Canaanites:

Now Deborah, a prophetess, the wife of Lapidoth, was judging Israel at that time. And she would sit under the palm tree of Deborah between Ramah and Bethel in the mountains of Ephraim. And the children of Israel came up to her for judgment. Then she sent and called for Barak the son of Abinoam from Kedesh in Naphtali, and said to him, "Has not the Lord God of Israel commanded, 'Go and deploy troops at Mount Tabor; take with you ten thousand men of the sons of Naphtali and of the sons of Zebulun; and against you I will deploy Sisera, the commander of Jabin's army, with his chariots and his multitude at the River Kishon; and I will deliver him into your hand'?"

And Barak said to her, "If you will go with me, then I will go; but if you will not go with me, I will not go!"

So she said, "I will surely go with you; nevertheless there will be no glory for you in the journey you are taking, for the Lord will sell Sisera into the hand of a woman. Then Deborah arose and went with Barak to Kedesh. And Barak called Zebulun and Naphtali to Kedesh; he went up with ten thousand men under his command, and Deborah went up with him.

Now Heber the Kenite, of the children of Hobab the father-in-law of Moses, had separated himself from the Kenites and pitched his tent near the terebinth tree at Zaanaim, which is beside Kedesh.

And they reported to Sisera that Barak the son of Abinoam had gone up to Mount Tabor. So Sisera gathered together all his chariots, nine hundred chariots of iron, and all the people who were with him, from Harosheth Hagoyim to the River Kishon.

Then Deborah said to Barak, "Up! For this is the day in which the Lord has delivered Sisera into your hand. Has not the Lord gone out before you?" So Barak went down from Mount Tabor with ten thousand men following him. And the Lord routed Sisera and all his chariots and all his army with the edge of the sword before Barak; and Sisera alighted from his chariot and fled away on foot. But Barak pursued the chariots and the army as far as Harosheth Hagoyim, and all the army of Sisera fell by the edge of the sword; not a man was left.

Judges 4:4-16

Lesson 6

God's Will:
The Ultimate Security

Then Deborah said to Barak, "Get ready!
This is the day the Lord will give you victory over Sisera,
for the Lord is marching ahead of you."
So Barak led his 10,000 warriors down the slopes
of Mount Tabor into battle.

Judges 4:14 NLT

THE LESSON

When God's will becomes your will, good things happen.

The Book of Judges (chapters 4 and 5) tells the story of Deborah, the fearless woman who guided Barak and helped lead the army of Israel to victory over the Canaanites. Deborah was a judge and a prophetess, a woman called by God to lead her people. And when she answered God's call, she was rewarded with one of the great victories of Old Testament times.

Like Deborah, all of us are called to serve our Creator. And, like Deborah, we may sometimes find ourselves facing trials that can bring trembling to the very depths of our souls. As believers, we must seek God's will and follow it. When we do, we are rewarded with victories, some great and some small. But when we turn away from God's will for our lives, we invite tragic consequences for ourselves and for those we love.

> To walk out of His will
> is to walk into nowhere.
>
> —
>
> *C. S. Lewis*

God has plans for all of us, but He will not force His plans upon us. To the contrary, He only makes His plans clear to those who genuinely and humbly seek His will.

As this day unfolds, seek God's will for your own life and obey His Word. When you entrust your life to Him completely and without reservation, He will give you the strength to meet any challenge, the courage to face any trial, and the wisdom to live in His righteousness and in His peace.

Something to Think about

When you place yourself in the center of God's will . . . He will provide for your needs and direct your path.

Absolute submission is not enough; we should go on to joyful acquiescence to the will of God.

C. H. Spurgeon

"If the Lord will" is not just a statement on a believer's lips; it is the constant attitude of his heart.

Warren Wiersbe

God is God. He knows what he is doing. When you can't trace his hand, trust his heart.

Max Lucado

Make God's will the focus of your life day by day. If you seek to please Him and Him alone, you'll find yourself satisfied with life.

Kay Arthur

Our sense of joy, satisfaction, and fulfillment in life increases, no matter what the circumstances, if we are in the center of God's will.

Billy Graham

The will of God is never exactly what you expect it to be. It may seem to be much worse, but in the end it's going to be a lot better and a lot bigger.

Elisabeth Elliot

Jesus yielded Himself to the Father's will. He was a model of "reverent submission." Jesus lived a life of prayer, faith, and obedience.

Shirley Dobson

When we come to Jesus stripped of pretensions, with a needy spirit, ready to listen, He meets us at the point of need.

Catherine Marshall

In the soul-searching of our lives, we are to stay quiet so we can hear Him say all that He wants to say to us in our hearts.

Charles Swindoll

MORE FROM GOD'S WORD

Commit your activities to the Lord and your plans will be achieved.

Proverbs 16:3 HCSB

And this world is fading away, along with everything it craves. But if you do the will of God, you will live forever.

1 John 2:17 NLT

Whoever does the will of God is My brother and sister and mother.

Mark 3:35 HCSB

However, each one must live his life in the situation the Lord assigned when God called him.

1 Corinthians 7:17 HCSB

O Lord, you have examined my heart and know everything about me. You know when I sit down or stand up. You know my every thought when far away. You chart the path ahead of me and tell me where to stop and rest.

Psalm 139:1-3 NLT

My Thoughts on This Lesson

_____

_____

_____

_____

_____

_____

_____

_____

_____

_____

A Prayer for Today

Lord, let Your will be my will. When I am confused,
give me maturity and wisdom. When I am worried, give me
courage and strength. Let me be Your faithful servant, Father,
always seeking Your guidance and Your will for my life.
Amen

Ruth

Ruth was a righteous woman who, despite difficult circumstances, remained faithful to her family and to her God. Ruth's life serves as a powerful example of faith, courage, and perseverance. In the chapters that follow, you will be asked to examine the details of Ruth's life, and you'll be asked to consider essential lessons you can learn from her story.

IMPORTANT EVENTS IN THE LIFE OF RUTH

○ Naomi, her husband Elimelech, and their two sons Mahlon and Kilion leave the town of Bethlehem during a famine. They travel to the country of Moab.

○ While living in the land of Moab, the sons marry two Moabite women, Ruth and Orpah.

○ Naomi's husband and sons die, leaving Naomi, Ruth, and Orpah widows.

○ Naomi instructs both her daughters-in-law to return to their mothers and find new husbands.

O Ruth refuses to leave Naomi; instead, she pledges to re-main with Naomi by telling her mother-in-law, "Wherever you go, I will go, and wherever you live, I will live; your people will be my people, and your God will be my God. Where you die, I will die, and there I will be buried."

O Naomi and Ruth travel to Bethlehem, a land that is famil-iar to Naomi but foreign to Ruth.

O Once she arrives in Bethlehem, Ruth doesn't delay or despair—she immediately goes to work gathering leftover pieces of grain in the fields of a man named Boaz.

O Boaz notices Ruth and encourages her to continue gather-ing in his fields.

O Naomi encourages Ruth to continue laboring in Boaz's fields. Naomi gives Ruth a plan for endearing herself to Boaz. Ruth follows Naomi's instructions, the plan works, and Boaz marries Ruth.

O Ruth gives birth to a child, Obed. Obed becomes the father of Jesse, the father of David. Thus, Ruth's life is an integral part of God's plans for the house of David. David's descendant Joseph wed Mary, the mother of Jesus.

Lesson 7

Where There Is Great Love, There Are Miracles

She said to them, "Each of you go back to your mother's home. May the Lord show faithful love to you as you have shown to the dead and to me. May the Lord enable each of you to find security in the house of your [new] husband." She kissed them, and they wept loudly.

Ruth 1:8-9 HCSB

THE LESSON

Ruth's story reminds us, yet again, that love conquers adversity.

After the death of her husband and sons, Naomi encouraged Ruth to move on with her life. After all, Ruth was still a young woman of marriageable age while Naomi was much older. But because of Ruth's love for Naomi, the younger woman refused to abandon her mother-in-law. So Ruth's story is not only a story about overcoming adversity; it is also a love story: love for God, love for Naomi, and love for Boaz.

Ruth demonstrated genuine love, and we should follow her example. Genuine love is loyal, patient, understanding, consistent, and considerate. Genuine love doesn't always spring up overnight, but it doesn't vanish overnight, either. And, genuine love requires effort. Simply put, if you wish to build lasting relationships, you must be willing to do your part.

God does not intend for you to experience mediocre relationships; He created you for far greater things. Building lasting relationships requires compassion, wisdom, empathy, kindness, courtesy, perseverance and forgiveness. If that sounds a lot like work, it is—which is perfectly fine with God.

> Prayer is the ultimate
> love language.
> It communicates
> in ways we can't.
>
> —
>
> *Stormie Omartian*

Why? Because He knows that you are capable of doing that work, and because He knows that the fruits of your labors will enrich the lives of your loved ones and the lives of generations yet unborn . . . just like Ruth.

Something to Think about

The key to successful Christian living lies in your submission to the Spirit of God. As a Christian, you are commanded to love people . . . and it's a commandment that applies to both saints and sinners.

If Jesus is the preeminent One in our lives, then we will love each other, submit to each other, and treat one another fairly in the Lord.

Warren Wiersbe

Those who abandon ship the first time it enters a storm miss the calm beyond. And the rougher the storms weathered together, the deeper and stronger real love grows.

Ruth Bell Graham

Love is an attribute of God. To love others is evidence of a genuine faith.

Kay Arthur

How do you spell love? When you reach the point where the happiness, security, and development of another person is as much of a driving force to you as your own happiness, security, and development, then you have a mature love. True love is spelled G-I-V-E. It is not based on what you can get, but rooted in what you can give to the other person.

Josh McDowell

Love must be supported and fed and protected, just like a little infant who is growing up at home.

James Dobson

Love is the seed of all hope. It is the enticement to trust, to risk, to try, and to go on.

Gloria Gaither

It is when we come to the Lord in our nothingness, our powerlessness and our helplessness that He then enables us to love in a way which, without Him, would be absolutely impossible.

Elisabeth Elliot

Hope looks for the good in people, opens doors for people, discovers what can be done to help, lights a candle, does not yield to cynicism. Hope sets people free.

Barbara Johnson

MORE FROM GOD'S WORD

I pray that you, being rooted and firmly established in love, may be able to comprehend with all the saints what is the breadth and width, height and depth, and to know the Messiah's love that surpasses knowledge, so you may be filled with all the fullness of God.

Ephesians 3:17-19 HCSB

If I speak the languages of men and of angels, but do not have love, I am a sounding gong or a clanging cymbal.

1 Corinthians 13:1 HCSB

Now these three remain: faith, hope, and love. But the greatest of these is love.

1 Corinthians 13:13 HCSB

Dear friends, if God loved us in this way, we also must love one another.

1 John 4:11 HCSB

We love because He first loved us.

1 John 4:19 HCSB

MY THOUGHTS ON THIS LESSON

_____

_____

_____

_____

_____

_____

_____

_____

_____

_____

A PRAYER FOR TODAY

Lord, You have given me the gift of love and You've asked me
to share it. The gift of love is a precious gift indeed.
Let me nurture love and treasure it. And, help me remember
that the essence of love is not to receive it, but to give it,
today and forever. Amen

Lesson 8

The Need for Humility

Ruth the Moabitess asked Naomi,
"Will you let me go into the fields and gather fallen grain
behind someone who allows me to?"
Ruth 2:2 HCSB

THE LESSON

Ruth was a humble worker in service of her family and her God. We, too, should be humble servants as we labor for the Master.

Ruth demonstrated a Christ-like attitude by humbling herself before God and before others. Gleaning leftover wheat was certainly not a glamorous job, yet Ruth was not too proud to work in that menial job. She understood her responsibility to Naomi, and she fulfilled it without fanfare.

Jesus teaches that the most esteemed men and women are not the self-congratulatory leaders of society but are instead the humblest of servants (like Ruth). But, as weak human beings, we sometimes fall short as we seek to puff ourselves up and glorify our own accomplishments. To do so is wrong.

> Humility expresses a genuine dependency on God and others.
>
> —
>
> *Charles Stanley*

Today, you may feel the temptation to build yourself up in the eyes of your neighbors. Resist that temptation. Instead, serve your neighbors quietly and without fanfare. Find a need and fill it . . . humbly. Lend a helping hand and share a word of kindness . . . anonymously. This is God's way.

As a humble servant, you will glorify yourself, not before men, but before God, and that's what God intends. After all, earthly glory is fleeting: here today and all too soon gone. But, heavenly glory endures throughout eternity. So, the choice is yours: Either you can lift yourself up here on earth and be humbled in heaven, or vice versa. Choose vice versa.

SOMETHING TO THINK ABOUT

God favors the humble just as surely as He disciplines the proud.

If you know who you are in Christ, your personal ego is not an issue.

Beth Moore

Jesus had a humble heart. If He abides in us, pride will never dominate our lives.

Billy Graham

Humility is the fairest and rarest flower that blooms.

Charles Swindoll

That's what I love about serving God. In His eyes, there are no little people . . . because there are no big people. We are all on the same playing field. We all start at square one. No one has it better than the other, or possesses unfair advantage.

Joni Eareckson Tada

All kindness and good deeds, we must keep silent. The result will be an inner reservoir of personality power.

Catherine Marshall

Let the love of Christ be believed in and felt in your hearts, and it will humble you.

C. H. Spurgeon

There is a canyon of difference between doing your best to glorify God and doing whatever it takes to glorify yourself. The quest for excellence is a mark of maturity. The quest for power is childish.

Max Lucado

Pride is the deification of self.

Oswald Chambers

Humility is a thing which must be genuine; the imitation of it is the nearest thing in the world to pride.

C. H. Spurgeon

MORE FROM GOD'S WORD

Clothe yourselves with humility toward one another, because God resists the proud, but gives grace to the humble.

1 Peter 5:5 HCSB

Humble yourselves therefore under the mighty hand of God, so that He may exalt you in due time, casting all your care upon Him, because He cares about you.

1 Peter 5:6-7 HCSB

But He said to me, "My grace is sufficient for you, for power is perfected in weakness." Therefore, I will most gladly boast all the more about my weaknesses, so that Christ's power may reside in me.

2 Corinthians 12:9 HCSB

You will save the humble people; but Your eyes are on the haughty, that You may bring them down.

2 Samuel 22:28 NKJV

If My people who are called by My name will humble themselves, and pray and seek My face, and turn from their wicked ways, then I will hear from heaven, and will forgive their sin and heal their land.

2 Chronicles 7:14 NKJV

MY THOUGHTS ON THIS LESSON

_____

_____

_____

_____

_____

_____

_____

_____

_____

_____

A PRAYER FOR TODAY

Heavenly Father, Jesus clothed Himself with humility when
He chose to leave heaven and come to earth to live and
die for us, His children. Jesus is my Master and my example.
Clothe me with humility, Lord, so that I might be more
like Your Son. Amen

Lesson 9

When You Trust God, You Experience His Peace

Come to Me, all you who are weary and burdened, and I will give you rest. Take My yoke upon you and learn from Me, because I am gentle and humble in heart, and you will find rest for your souls. For My yoke is easy and My burden is light.

Matthew 11:28–30 HCSB

THE LESSON

Because Ruth trusted God, and because she obeyed Him, she ultimately experienced God's peace. We, too, can experience His peace when we trust and obey.

Because she trusted God and followed His peace, Ruth received the Father's blessings, and she must have experienced His peace. Have you found the lasting peace that can—and should—be yours when you follow God's path? Or are you still chasing the illusion of "peace and happiness" that the world promises but cannot deliver?

The beautiful words of John 14:27 promise that Jesus offers peace, not as the world gives, but as He alone gives: "Peace I leave with you. My peace I give to you. I do not give to you as the world gives. Your heart must not be troubled or fearful" (HCSB). Your challenge is to accept Christ's peace into your heart and then, as best you can, to share His peace with your neighbors. But sometimes, that's easier said than done.

> You will get untold flak for prioritizing God's revealed and present will for your life over man's . . . but, boy, is it worth it.
>
> —
>
> *Beth Moore*

If you are a person with lots of obligations and plenty of responsibilities, it is simply a fact of life: You worry. From time to time, you worry about finances, safety, health, home, family, or about countless other concerns, some great and some small. Where is the best place to take your worries? Take them to God . . . and leave them there.

The Scottish preacher George McDonald observed, "It has been well said that no man ever sank under the burden of the day. It is when tomorrow's burden is added to the burden of today that the weight is more than a man can bear. Never load yourselves so, my friends. If you find yourselves so loaded, at least remember this: it is your own doing, not God's. He begs you to leave the future to Him."

Today, as a gift to yourself, to your family, and to your friends, claim the inner peace that is your spiritual birthright: the peace of Jesus Christ. Christ is standing at the door, waiting patiently for you to invite Him to reign over your heart. His eternal peace is offered freely. Claim it today.

SOMETHING TO THINK ABOUT

God's peace surpasses human understanding. When you accept His peace, your life will be forever changed.

To know God as He really is—in His essential nature and character—is to arrive at a citadel of peace that circumstances may storm, but can never capture.

Catherine Marshall

That peace, which has been described and which believers enjoy, is a participation of the peace which their glorious Lord and Master himself enjoys.

Jonathan Edwards

The fruit of our placing all things in God's hands is the presence of His abiding peace in our hearts.

Hannah Whitall Smith

There may be no trumpet sound or loud applause when we make a right decision, just a calm sense of resolution and peace.

Gloria Gaither

A great many people are trying to make peace, but that has already been done. God has not left it for us to do; all we have to do is to enter into it.

D. L. Moody

MORE FROM GOD'S WORD

God has called us to peace.

1 Corinthians 7:15 NKJV

Be of good comfort, be of one mind, live in peace; and the God of love and peace will be with you.

2 Corinthians 13:11 NKJV

For He is our peace.

Ephesians 2:14 HCSB

The result of righteousness will be peace; the effect of righteousness will be quiet confidence forever.

Isaiah 32:17 HCSB

I have told you these things so that in Me you may have peace. In the world you have suffering. But take courage! I have conquered the world.

John 16:33 HCSB

My Thoughts on This Lesson

_____

_____

_____

_____

_____

_____

_____

_____

_____

_____

A Prayer for Today

The world talks about peace, but only You, Lord, can give
a perfect and lasting peace. True peace comes through
the Prince of Peace, and His peace passes all understanding.
Help me to accept His peace—and share it—
this day and forever. Amen

Lesson 10

Hard Work Is Rewarded

*She asked, "Will you let me gather fallen grain among
the bundles behind the harvesters?"
She came and has remained from early morning until
now, except that she rested a little in the shelter.*

Ruth 2:7 HCSB

THE LESSON

Ruth was diligent in her work . . . we should be diligent in
ours.

Ruth knew that Naomi could not provide for their needs, so Ruth rolled up her sleeves and went to work gathering food in the fields. We, like Ruth, should be willing workers as we care for our loved ones and ourselves.

The old adage is both familiar and true: We must pray as if everything depended upon God, but work as if everything depended upon us. Yet sometimes, when we are weary and discouraged, we may allow our worries to sap our energy and our hope. God has other intentions. God intends that we pray for things, and He intends that we be willing to work for the things that we pray for. More importantly, God intends that our work should become His work.

Your success in life will depend, in large part, upon the passion that you bring to your work. God has created a world in which diligence is rewarded and sloth is not. So whatever you choose to do, do it with commitment, with excitement, with enthusiasm, and with vigor.

> We must trust as if it all depended on God and work as if it all depended on us.
>
> —
>
> *C. H. Spurgeon*

It has been said that there are no shortcuts to any place worth going. And for believers, it's important to remember that hard work is not simply a proven way to get ahead, it's also part of God's plan for His children.

God did not create you to be ordinary; He created you for far greater things. Reaching for greater things usually requires work and lots of it, which is perfectly fine with God. After all, He knows that you're up to the task, and He has big plans for you. Very big plans . . .

SOMETHING TO THINK ABOUT

When you find work that pleases God—and when you apply yourself conscientiously to the job at hand—you'll be rewarded.

The world does not consider labor a blessing, therefore it flees and hates it, but the pious who fear the Lord labor with a ready and cheerful heart, for they know God's command, and they acknowledge His calling.

Martin Luther

Ordinary work, which is what most of us do most of the time, is ordained by God every bit as much as is the extraordinary.

Elisabeth Elliot

Thank God every morning when you get up that you have something which must be done, whether you like it or not. Work breeds a hundred virtues that idleness never knows.

Charles Kingsley

It may be that the day of judgment will dawn tomorrow; in that case, we shall gladly stop working for a better tomorrow. But not before.

Dietrich Bonhoeffer

Although God causes all things to work together for good for His children, He still holds us accountable for our behavior.

Kay Arthur

MORE FROM GOD'S WORD

Whatever you do, do it enthusiastically, as something done for the Lord and not for men.

Colossians 3:23 HCSB

Whatever your hands find to do, do with [all] your strength.

Ecclesiastes 9:10 HCSB

He did it with all his heart. So he prospered.

2 Chronicles 31:21 NKJV

Don't work only while being watched, in order to please men, but as slaves of Christ, do God's will from your heart. Render service with a good attitude, as to the Lord and not to men.

Ephesians 6:6-7 HCSB

We must do the works of Him who sent Me while it is day. Night is coming when no one can work.

John 9:4 HCSB

My Thoughts on This Lesson

_____

_____

_____

_____

_____

_____

_____

_____

A Prayer for Today

Lord, I know that You desire a bountiful harvest for all
Your children. But, You have instructed us that we must sow
before we reap, not after. Help me, Lord, to sow the seeds of
Your abundance everywhere I go. Let me be diligent in all my
undertakings and give me patience to wait for Your harvest.
In time, Lord, let me reap the harvest that is found in
Your will for my life. Amen

Lesson 11

You Can Overcome Adversity

"I left full, but the Lord has brought me back empty.
Why do you call me Naomi,
since the Lord has pronounced [judgment] on me,
and the Almighty has afflicted me?"

Ruth 1:21 HCSB

THE LESSON

Ruth's story teaches us that adversity is temporary, and that God has plans for us that we cannot see.

Ruth endured tragedies that would have destroyed a lesser woman. She experienced famine and the loss of her husband. In response to her losses, she might have abandoned hope, and she might have abandoned her mother-in-law Naomi. But Ruth did neither. Instead, she remained faithful to Naomi and to God. And in time, Ruth was blessed because of her faithfulness.

Have you experienced a recent heartache? Does your future seem foreboding? Are you anxious about your finances, your health, or your relationships? If so, you must turn your concerns over to a power far greater than your own.

> A Christian is never in a state of completion but always in the process of becoming.
>
> —
>
> *Martin Luther*

The Bible teaches us that we need never carry our burdens alone. God is always there, always available, always willing to give us protection, comfort, and support . . . if we let Him. Yet sometimes, we may find it difficult to trust the Creator. Why? Because we are imperfect mortals who possess imperfect faith—and because of our doubts, we may be slow to trust our Heavenly Father.

The next time you face a difficult situation or a tough decision, give your burdens to God. He has promised to carry them, and He will keep that promise. Your job, simply put, is to let go and to give your troubles to the Father. When you do, you'll be protected because God can bear any burden and tackle any trouble. No problem is too big for Him, including yours.

Something to Think about

During tough times, work as if everything depended on you and pray as if everything depended on God.

God will never let you sink under your circumstances. He always provides a safety net and His love always encircles.

Barbara Johnson

If you learn to trust God with a child-like dependence on Him as your loving heavenly Father, no trouble can destroy you.

Billy Graham

The vigor of our spiritual lives will be in exact proportion to the place held by the Bible in our lives and in our thoughts.

George Mueller

Measure the size of the obstacles against the size of God.

Beth Moore

The sermon of your life in tough times ministers to people more powerfully than the most eloquent speaker.

Bill Bright

The only way to learn a strong faith is to endure great trials. I have learned my faith by standing firm amid the most severe of tests.

George Mueller

God's plan for our guidance is for us to grow gradually in wisdom before we get to the crossroads.

Bill Hybels

We look at our burdens and heavy loads, and we shrink from them. But, if we lift them and bind them about our hearts, they become wings, and on them we can rise and soar toward God.

Mrs. Charles E. Cowman

God whispers to us in our pleasures, speaks in our conscience, but shouts in our pain.

C. S. Lewis

More from God's Word

We are pressured in every way but not crushed; we are perplexed but not in despair.

2 Corinthians 4:8 HCSB

I will be with you when you pass through the waters . . . when you walk through the fire . . . the flame will not burn you. For I the Lord your God, the Holy One of Israel, and your Savior.

Isaiah 43:2-3 HCSB

Consider it a great joy, my brothers, whenever you experience various trials, knowing that the testing of your faith produces endurance. But endurance must do its complete work, so that you may be mature and complete, lacking nothing.

James 1:2-4 HCSB

When you are in distress and all these things have happened to you, you will return to the Lord your God in later days and obey Him. He will not leave you, destroy you, or forget the covenant with your fathers that He swore to them by oath, because the Lord your God is a compassionate God.

Deuteronomy 4:30-31 HCSB

MY THOUGHTS ON THIS LESSON

_____

_____

_____

_____

_____

_____

_____

_____

_____

_____

A PRAYER FOR TODAY

Heavenly Father, You are my strength and refuge. I can face
the difficulties of this day because You are with me. You are
my light and pathway. As I follow You, Father, I can overcome
adversity just as Jesus overcame this world. Amen

Lesson 12

When Faced with an Important Decision, Let God Help You Choose

But Ruth replied: "Do not persuade me to leave you or go back and not follow you. For wherever you go, I will go, and wherever you live, I will live; your people will be my people, and your God will be my God. Where you die, I will die, and there I will be buried. May the Lord do this to me, and even more, if anything but death separates you and me."

Ruth 1:16-17 HCSB

THE LESSON

Ruth faced choices, and so do we. Ruth chose wisely, and so must we.

Ruth's decision to remain loyal to Naomi reflected an understanding of God's desire for Ruth's life. Ruth's decision reflected God's will; our decisions should, too.

Life is a series of choices. From the instant we wake in the morning until the moment we nod off to sleep at night, we make countless decisions: decisions about the things we do, decisions about the words we speak, and decisions about the thoughts we choose to think. Simply put, the quality of those decisions determines the quality of our lives.

As believers who have been saved by a loving and merciful God, we have every reason to make wise choices. Yet sometimes, amid the inevitable hustle and bustle of life here on earth, we allow ourselves to behave in ways that we know are displeasing to God. When we do, we forfeit—albeit temporarily—the joy and the peace that we might otherwise experience through Him.

As you consider the next step in your life's journey, take time to consider how many things in this life you can control: your thoughts, your words, your priorities, and your actions, for starters. And then, if you sincerely want to discover God's purpose for your life, make choices that are pleasing to Him.

SOMETHING TO THINK ABOUT

Every step of your life's journey is a choice . . . and the quality of those choices determines the quality of the journey.

God is voting for us all the time. The devil is voting against us all the time. The way we vote carries the election.

Corrie ten Boom

The disciple who abides in Jesus is in the will of God, and his apparently free choices are God's foreordained decrees. Mysterious? Logically contradictory and absurd? Yes, but a glorious truth to a saint.

Oswald Chambers

We are either the masters or the victims of our attitudes. It is a matter of personal choice. Who we are today is the result of choices we made yesterday. Tomorrow, we will become what we choose today. To change means to choose to change.

John Maxwell

No matter how many books you read, no matter how many schools you attend, you're never really wise until you start making wise choices.

Marie T. Freeman

There may be no trumpet sound or loud applause when we make a right decision, just a calm sense of resolution and peace.

Gloria Gaither

Life is pretty much like a cafeteria line—it offers us many choices, both good and bad. The Christian must have a spiritual radar that detects the difference not only between bad and good but also among good, better, and best.

Dennis Swanberg

Faith is not a feeling; it is action. It is a willed choice.

Elisabeth Elliot

Knowing God involves an intimate, personal relationship that is developed over time through prayer and getting answers to prayer, through Bible study and applying its teaching to our lives, through obedience and experiencing the power of God, through moment-by-moment submission to Him that results in a moment-by-moment filling of the Holy Spirit.

Anne Graham Lotz

We had plenty of challenges, some of which were tremendously serious, yet God has enabled us to walk, crawl, limp, or leap—whatever way we could progress—toward wholeness.

Beth Moore

Life is a gift from God, and we must treasure it, protect it, and invest it.

Warren Wiersbe

MORE FROM GOD'S WORD

Lord, You light my lamp; my God illuminates my darkness.

Psalm 18:28 HCSB

I will instruct you and teach you in the way you should go; I will guide you with My eye.

Psalm 32:8 NKJV

Yet Lord, You are our Father; we are the clay, and You are our potter; we all are the work of Your hands.

Isaiah 64:8 HCSB

Teach me Your way, Lord, and I will live by Your truth. Give me an undivided mind to fear Your name.

Psalm 86:11 HCSB

Teach me to do Your will, for You are my God. May Your gracious Spirit lead me on level ground.

Psalm 143:10 HCSB

My Thoughts on This Lesson

_____

_____

_____

_____

_____

_____

_____

_____

_____

_____

A Prayer for Today

Heavenly Father, I have many choices to make.
Help me choose wisely as I follow in the footsteps of
Your only begotten Son. Amen

Lesson 13

Prayer Moves Mountains

So I say to you, keep asking, and it will be given to you.
Keep searching, and you will find.
Keep knocking, and the door will be opened to you.

Luke 11:9 HCSB

THE LESSON

Ruth was a godly woman who surely understood the power of prayer. We, too, should understand the importance of asking God for the things we need.

How often do you ask God for His help and His wisdom? Occasionally? Intermittently? Whenever you experience a crisis? Hopefully not. Hopefully, you've acquired the habit of asking for God's assistance early and often. And hopefully, you have learned to seek His guidance in every aspect of your life.

The Bible promises that God will guide you if you let Him. Your job is to let Him. But sometimes, you will be tempted to do otherwise. Sometimes, you'll be tempted to go along with the crowd; other times, you'll be tempted to do things your way, not God's way. When you feel those temptations, resist them.

God has promised that when you ask for His help, He will not withhold it. So ask. Ask Him to meet the needs of your day. Ask Him to lead you, to protect you, and to correct you. And trust the answers He gives.

God stands at the door and waits. When you knock, He opens. When you ask, He answers. Your task, of course, is to seek His guidance prayerfully, confidently, and often.

SOMETHING TO THINK ABOUT

When you ask God for His assistance, He hears your request—and in His own time, He will answer.

All we have to do is to acknowledge our need, move from self-sufficiency to dependence, and ask God to become our hiding place.

Bill Hybels

Some people think God does not like to be troubled with our constant asking. But, the way to trouble God is not to come at all.

D. L. Moody

Don't be afraid to ask your heavenly Father for anything you need. Indeed, nothing is too small for God's attention or too great for his power.

Dennis Swanberg

When will we realize that we're not troubling God with our questions and concerns? His heart is open to hear us—his touch nearer than our next thought—as if no one in the world existed but us. Our very personal God wants to hear from us personally.

Gigi Graham Tchividjian

Whatever may be our circumstances in life, may each one of us really believe that by way of the Throne we have unlimited power.

Annie Armstrong

When you ask God to do something, don't ask timidly; put your whole heart into it.

Marie T. Freeman

By asking in Jesus' name, we're making a request not only in His authority, but also for His interests and His benefit.

Shirley Dobson

Prayer moves the arm that moves the world.

Annie Armstrong

We need never shout across the spaces to an absent God. He is nearer than our own soul, closer than our most secret thoughts.

A. W. Tozer

I need the spiritual revival that comes from spending quiet time alone with Jesus in prayer and in thoughtful meditation on His Word.

Anne Graham Lotz

MORE FROM GOD'S WORD

If you remain in Me and My words remain in you, ask whatever you want and it will be done for you.

John 15:7 HCSB

What father among you, if his son asks for a fish, will, instead of a fish, give him a snake? Or if he asks for an egg, will give him a scorpion? If you then, who are evil, know how to give good gifts to your children, how much more will the heavenly Father give the Holy Spirit to those who ask Him?

Luke 11:11-13 HCSB

And in that day you will ask Me nothing. Most assuredly, I say to you, whatever you ask the Father in My name He will give you. Until now you have asked nothing in My name. Ask, and you will receive, that your joy may be full.

John 16:23-24 NKJV

Don't worry about anything, but in everything, through prayer and petition with thanksgiving, let your requests be made known to God.

Philippians 4:6 HCSB

If you really carry out the royal law prescribed in Scripture, You shall love your neighbor as yourself, you are doing well.

James 2:8 HCSB

MY THOUGHTS ON THIS LESSON

_____

_____

_____

_____

_____

_____

_____

_____

_____

_____

A PRAYER FOR TODAY

Lord, I pray to You because You desire it and because I need it.
Prayer not only changes things, it also changes me. Help me,
Lord, never to face the demands of the day without first spending
time with You, and help me to make prayer a part of everything
that I do and everything that I am. Amen

Lesson 14

The Importance of Character

"Now don't be afraid, my daughter. I will do for you whatever you say, since all the people in my town know that you are a woman of noble character."

Ruth 3:11 HCSB

THE LESSON

Because Ruth was known as a woman of integrity, Boaz looked upon her with favor.

Ruth's integrity was evident to all, including Boaz. In Ruth's day, character counted, and it still does.

Catherine Marshall correctly observed, "The single most important element in any human relationship is honesty—with oneself, with God, and with others." Godly men and women agree. As believers in Christ, we must seek to live each day with discipline, honesty, and faith. When we do, at least two things happen: integrity becomes a habit, and God blesses us because of our obedience to Him. Living a life of integrity isn't always the easiest way, but it is always the right way . . . and God clearly intends that it should be our way, too.

> Character is what
> you are in the dark.
>
> —
>
> D. L. Moody

Character isn't built overnight; it is built slowly over a lifetime. It is the sum of every right decision and every honest word. It is forged on the anvil of honorable work and polished by the twin virtues of honesty and fairness. Character is a precious thing—difficult to build and wonderful to behold.

Oswald Chambers, the author of the Christian classic, My Utmost for His Highest, advised, "Never support an experience which does not have God as its source, and faith in God as its result." These words serve as a powerful reminder that as Christians we are called to walk with God and to obey His commandments. But, we live in a world that presents us with countless temptations to wander far from God's path. These temptations have the potential to destroy us, in part, because they cause us to be dishonest with ourselves and with others.

Dishonesty is a habit. Once we start bending the truth, we're likely to keep bending it. A far better strategy, of course, is to acquire the habit of being completely forthright with God, with other people, and with ourselves.

Honesty is also a habit, a habit that pays powerful dividends for those who place character above convenience. So, the next time you're tempted to bend the truth—or to break it—ask yourself this simple question: "What does God want me to do?" Then listen carefully to your conscience. When you do, your actions will be honorable, and your character will take care of itself.

SOMETHING TO THINK ABOUT

When your words are honest and your intentions are pure, you have nothing to fear. Ruth maintained her integrity, and so must you.

Image is what people think we are; integrity is what we really are.

John Maxwell

There is something about having endured great loss that brings purity of purpose and strength of character.

Barbara Johnson

What lessons about honor did you learn from your childhood? Are you living what you learned today?

Dennis Swanberg

Our life pursuits will reflect our character and personal integrity.

Franklin Graham

Character means living your life before God, fearing only Him, and seeking to please Him alone, no matter how you feel or what others may say or do.

Warren Wiersbe

It's sobering to contemplate how much time, effort, sacrifice, compromise, and attention we give to acquiring and increasing our supply of something that is totally insignificant in eternity.

Anne Graham Lotz

MORE FROM GOD'S WORD

As the water reflects the face, so the heart reflects the person.

Proverbs 27:19 HCSB

We also rejoice in our afflictions, because we know that affliction produces endurance, endurance produces proven character, and proven character produces hope.

Romans 5:3-4 HCSB

A good name is to be chosen rather than great riches, loving favor rather than silver and gold.

Proverbs 22:1 NKJV

Do not be deceived: "Evil company corrupts good habits."

1 Corinthians 15:33 NKJV

In all things showing yourself to be a pattern of good works; in doctrine showing integrity, reverence, incorruptibility . . . .

Titus 2:7 NKJV

My Thoughts on This Lesson

_____

_____

_____

_____

_____

_____

_____

_____

_____

_____

A Prayer for Today

Dear Lord, every day can be an exercise in character-building, and that's what I intend to make this day. I will be mindful that my thoughts and actions have great consequences, consequences in my own life and in the lives of my loved ones. I will strive to make my thoughts and actions pleasing to You, so that I may be an instrument of Your peace, today and every day. Amen

Lesson 15

The Value of Loyalty

*"May the Lord do this to me, and even more,
if anything but death separates you and me."*

Ruth 1:17 HCSB

THE LESSON

Ruth was loyal to Naomi . . . and Ruth's loyalty was rewarded.
We, too, are rewarded when we remain loyal to our friends
and loved ones.

Loyalty is another quality Ruth exhibited in her relationship to Naomi. Loyalty is the glue that holds relationships, families, and societies together. When we make loyalty the hallmark of our dealings with others, we reap lasting rewards. But when we forget a friend or family member—or when we betray a trust—we invite consequences that are both troubling and predictable.

We live in a world that seems to be paying less and less attention to the ties that bind. Ours is a highly mobile society; we move from job to job, from relationship to relationship, from town to town. But loyalty has not gone out of style, and it never will. Loyalty is a sacred trust.

May we all behave accordingly.

SOMETHING TO THINK ABOUT

When you are loyal to your family and friends—when you treat them in the same way that you would want to be treated—you'll earn respect from your loved ones and blessings from your Father in heaven.

The greatest ability is dependability.

Vance Havner

The best times in life are made a thousand times better when shared with a dear friend.

Luci Swindoll

Any time you make a commitment to something, it will be tested.

John Maxwell

God wants to teach us that when we commit our lives to Him, He gives us that wonderful teacher, the Holy Spirit.

Gloria Gaither

I have found that the closer I am to the godly people around me, the easier it is for me to live a righteous life because they hold me accountable.

John MacArthur

We become whatever we are committed to.

Rick Warren

God is able to do anything He pleases with one ordinary person fully consecrated to Him.

Henry Blackaby and Claude King

Commitment doesn't come easy, but when you're fighting for something you believe in, the struggle is worth it.

John Maxwell

God calls us to be committed to Him, to be committed to making a difference, and to be committed to reconciliation.

Bill Hybels

Integrity is the glue that holds our way of life together. We must constantly strive to keep our integrity intact. When wealth is lost, nothing is lost; when health is lost, something is lost; when character is lost, all is lost.

Billy Graham

MORE FROM GOD'S WORD

Oil and incense bring joy to the heart, and the sweetness of a friend is better than self-counsel.

Proverbs 27:9 HCSB

Beloved, if God so loved us, we also ought to love one another.

1 John 4:11 NKJV

A friend loves at all times, and a brother is born for a difficult time.

Proverbs 17:17 HCSB

I thank my God upon every remembrance of you.

Philippians 1:3 NKJV

Ye shall not steal, neither deal falsely, neither lie one to another.

Leviticus 19:11 KJV

MY THOUGHTS ON THIS LESSON

_____

_____

_____

_____

_____

_____

_____

_____

_____

A PRAYER FOR TODAY

Dear Lord, make me a person of unwavering loyalty to You
and to my family. Guide me away from the temptations and
distractions of this world, so that I might honor You with my
thoughts, my actions, and my prayers. Amen

Esther

Esther was a courageous woman who used her intelligence and her natural beauty to save the Jewish people. Esther's life serves as a powerful example of faith, planning, and self-confidence.

In the chapters that follow, you will be asked to examine the detail of Esther's life, and you'll be asked to consider essential lessons you can glean from her story.

KEY EVENTS IN THE LIFE OF ESTHER

○ Esther is an orphan girl living in the city of Shushan, the capital of Persia. She is raised by her cousin Mordecai, a relatively minor official in the king's palace. Mordecai treats Esther as a daughter. Both Esther and Mordecai are Jews.

○ Queen Vashti of Persia disobeys her husband, King Xerxes. Vashti is banished by the king who then begins a search for a new queen. He summons the most beautiful women from his empire to form a royal harem. One of those women is Esther, who has matured into a beautiful young maiden.

○ King Xerxes finds Esther to be the most pleasing woman in his entire kingdom. He makes her his queen.

○ Mordecai thwarts a plot to assassinate King Xerxes. But Mordecai receives little recognition for his loyalty and bravery. King Xerxes is unaware that Mordecai has saved his life.

○ A power-hungry, self-serving official named Haman is named second-in-command to the king. Haman insists that Mordecai bow down in tribute, but Mordecai refuses. Haman is furious; he forms a plot to kill Mordecai along with all the other Jews in Persia.

○ Haman deceives Xerxes and convinces the king to condemn all people to death who "do not obey the king's laws." When the king gives Haman his approval, Haman secretly intends to kill all Jews, and a day is chosen for the executions to take place.

○ Mordecai tells Queen Esther of the King's decree, and she makes the decision to risk her own life to save her people.

○ As part of her plan, Esther invites both King Xerxes and Haman to a banquet. At the banquet, the king asks Esther what she wants from him. He promises to give her anything, but Esther simply invites both men to a second banquet the following night, when she will answer the king's question.

○ At the advice of his wife and friends, Haman builds a tall gallows to hang his enemy Mordecai. Then, Haman goes to the king's court to receive permission to hang the queen's cousin.

○ Meanwhile, after the first banquet, the king cannot sleep; as he reviews royal records, he discovers information about the assassination plot against him and Mordecai's role in thwarting the plot. The king asks Haman what should be done to reward great heroes, and the ever-vain Haman misunderstands the king's intent—Haman believes that it is himself, not Mordecai, whom the king intends to reward. So Haman describes a rich reward, and the king agrees. Then, the king informs Haman that it is Mordecai who will be honored, and Haman is terribly distressed.

○ The following night, at the second banquet, the king intends to grant Esther's wish, so he asks her what she wants. Esther asks that her people, the Jews, be spared from death, because she and her people have been condemned to die by a certain man, Haman.

O Upon hearing the entire story, and as a result of Esther's request, the king is indeed outraged. He condemns Haman to death and has him hanged on the same high gallows that Haman had built for Mordecai.

O The king gives Esther Haman's entire estate. Because of Esther's courage, and because she seizes the opportunity God has placed before her, the Jews are saved.

Lesson 16

You Can Live Courageously

"I will go to the king even if it is against the law. If I perish, I perish."

Esther 4:16 HCSB

THE LESSON

Esther behaved courageously, and we should do likewise.

King Xerxes of Persia banished Queen Vashti and began the search for a new queen. Esther, a beautiful Jewish girl was the king's choice to assume the throne. Later, the king's second-in-command, an evil man named Haman, devised a plot to murder all the Jews in Persia. Esther placed her own life at risk in order to save her people.

The story of Esther is a story of courage. Despite the dangers she faced, Queen Esther took decisive action. We should do likewise.

Every life (including yours) is an unfolding series of events: some fabulous, some not-so-fabulous, and some downright disheartening. When you reach the mountaintops of life, it isn't hard to be brave. But, when the storm clouds form overhead, your faith will be tested, sometimes to the breaking point. As a believer, you can take comfort in this fact: Wherever you find yourself, whether at the top of the mountain or the depths of the valley, God is there, and because He cares for you, you can live courageously.

Christians have every reason to be courageous. After all, the ultimate battle has already been fought and won on the cross at Calvary. But, even dedicated followers of Christ may find their courage tested by the inevitable disappointments and tragedies that occur in the lives of believers and nonbelievers alike.

> There comes a time when we simply have to face the challenges in our lives and stop backing down.
>
> —
>
> *John Eldredge*

The next time you find your courage tested to the limit, remember that God is as near as your next breath, and remember that He is your shield and your strength; He is your protector and your deliverer. Call upon Him in your hour of need and then be comforted. Whatever your challenge, whatever your trouble, God can handle it. And will.

SOMETHING TO THINK ABOUT

With God as your partner, you have nothing to fear. Why? Because you and God, working together, can handle absolutely anything that comes your way.

Jesus Christ can make the weakest man into a divine dreadnought, fearing nothing.

Oswald Chambers

Faith not only can help you through a crisis, it can help you to approach life after the hard times with a whole new perspective. It can help you adopt an outlook of hope and courage through faith to face reality.

John Maxwell

Take courage. We walk in the wilderness today and in the Promised Land tomorrow.

D. L. Moody

Just as courage is faith in good, so discouragement is faith in evil, and, while courage opens the door to good, discouragement opens it to evil.

Hannah Whitall Smith

If a person fears God, he or she has no reason to fear anything else. On the other hand, if a person does not fear God, then fear becomes a way of life.

Beth Moore

More from God's Word

Be strong and courageous, and do the work. Don't be afraid or discouraged, for the Lord God, my God, is with you. He won't leave you or forsake you.

1 Chronicles 28:20 HCSB

But when Jesus heard it, He answered him, "Don't be afraid. Only believe."

Luke 8:50 HCSB

For God has not given us a spirit of fearfulness, but one of power, love, and sound judgment.

2 Timothy 1:7 HCSB

Be alert, stand firm in the faith, be brave and strong.

1 Corinthians 16:13 HCSB

But He said to them, "Why are you fearful, you of little faith?" Then He got up and rebuked the winds and the sea. And there was a great calm.

Matthew 8:26 HCSB

MY THOUGHTS ON THIS LESSON

_____

_____

_____

_____

_____

_____

_____

_____

_____

A PRAYER FOR TODAY

Dear Lord, fill me with Your Spirit and help me face my
challenges with courage and determination. Keep me mindful,
Father, that You are with me always—and with You by my side,
I have nothing to fear. Amen

Lesson 17

God Has a Plan for Your Life, and You Can Discover It

Yet Lord, You are our Father;
we are the clay, and You are our potter;
we all are the work of Your hands.

Isaiah 64:8 HCSB

THE LESSON

Esther discovered God's will for her life; we, too, should seek God's will for our lives.

God had big plans for Esther, and He gave her all the tools she needed to succeed: She possessed beauty, intelligence, courage, and common sense. And when the time came for Esther to follow the path God had chosen for her, she did not hesitate. And neither should we.

Perhaps you're asking yourself if God really has a plan for your life. Of course He does! He is trying to lead you along a path of His choosing . . . but He won't force you to follow. God has given you free will, the opportunity to make decisions for yourself: the choice to obey God's Word and to seek His will is yours and yours alone.

When you make the decision to seek God's will for your life— and you should—then you will contemplate His Word, and you will be watchful for His signs. You will associate with fellow believers who will encourage your spiritual growth. And, you will listen to that inner voice that speaks to you in the quiet moments of your daily devotionals.

> Absolute submission
> is not enough;
> we should go on to joyful
> acquiescence to the
> will of God.
>
> —
>
> C. H. *Spurgeon*

Yes, God does indeed have a plan for you; He intends to use you in wonderful, unexpected ways if you let Him. But be forewarned: the decision to seek God's plan and fulfill His purpose is ultimately a decision that you must make by yourself and for yourself. The consequences of that decision have implications that are both profound and eternal, so choose carefully. And then, as you go about your daily activities, keep your eyes and ears open, as well as your heart, because God is patiently trying to get His message through . . . and there's no better moment than this one for you to help Him.

SOMETHING TO THINK ABOUT

When you place yourself in the center of God's will, He will provide for your needs and direct your path.

Our sense of joy, satisfaction, and fulfillment in life increases, no matter what the circumstances, if we are in the center of God's will.

Billy Graham

The will of God is never exactly what you expect it to be. It may seem to be much worse, but in the end it's going to be a lot better and a lot bigger.

Elisabeth Elliot

Jesus yielded Himself to the Father's will. He was a model of "reverent submission." Jesus lived a life of prayer, faith, and obedience.

Shirley Dobson

To walk out of His will is to walk into nowhere.

C. S. Lewis

The center of power is not to be found in summit meetings or in peace conferences. It is not in Peking or Washington or the United Nations, but rather where a child of God prays in the power of the Spirit for God's will to be done in her life, in her home, and in the world around her.

Ruth Bell Graham

MORE FROM GOD'S WORD

For it is better to suffer for doing good, if that should be God's will, than for doing evil.

1 Peter 3:17 HCSB

He is the Lord. He will do what He thinks is good.

1 Samuel 3:18 HCSB

For this reason we also, since the day we heard it, do not cease to pray for you, and to ask that you may be filled with the knowledge of His will in all wisdom and spiritual understanding.

Colossians 1:9 NKJV

Naked I came from my mother's womb, and naked I will leave this life. The Lord gives, and the Lord takes away. Praise the name of the Lord.

Job 1:21 HCSB

Father, if You are willing, take this cup away from Me—nevertheless, not My will, but Yours, be done.

Luke 22:42 HCSB

My Thoughts on This Lesson

_____

_____

_____

_____

_____

_____

_____

_____

_____

_____

A Prayer for Today

Heavenly Father, in these quiet moments before this busy day
unfolds, I come to You. I will study Your Word and seek
Your guidance. Give me the wisdom to know Your will for my life
and the courage to follow wherever You may lead me,
today and forever. Amen

Lesson 18

It Pays to Plan

"If it pleases the king," Esther replied,
*"may the king and Haman come today to the banquet
I have prepared for them."*

Esther 5:4 HCSB

THE LESSON

Careful planning increases the chances of success.

After seeking God's guidance through prayer and fasting, Esther developed a plan which ultimately saved her people. God expects us to pray, of course. But He also expects us to plan carefully. And He expects us to work diligently to make our plans come true.

It has been said that it is as important to have holes in our shoes from working God's plan as it is to have holes in the knees of our pants from kneeling in prayer. Both prayer and planning are necessary.

Are you willing to plan for the future—and are you willing to work diligently to accomplish the plans that you've made? If you desire to reap a bountiful harvest from life, you should plan for the future (by crafting a "to-do list for life") while entrusting the final outcome to God. Then, you should do your part to make the future better (by working dutifully), while acknowledging the sovereignty of God's hands over all affairs, including your own.

As you make plans and establish priorities, remember this: you're not the only one working on your behalf: God, too, is at work. And with Him as your partner, your ultimate success is guaranteed.

God has big plans for your life, wonderful, surprising plans . . . but He won't force those plans upon you. To the contrary, He has given you free will, the ability to make decisions on your own. Now, it's up to you to make those decisions wisely.

If you seek to live in accordance with God's plan for your life, you will study His Word, you will be attentive to His instructions, and you will be watchful for His signs. You will associate with fellow believers who, by their words and actions, will encourage your spiritual growth. You will assiduously avoid those two terrible temptations: the temptation to sin and the temptation to squander time. And finally, you will listen carefully, even reverently, to the conscience that God has placed in your heart.

God intends to use you in wonderful, unexpected ways if you let Him. Your job, of course, is to let Him.

Something to Think about

Think ahead—it's the best way of making sure you don't get left behind.

The only way you can experience abundant life is to surrender your plans to Him.

Charles Stanley

Allow your dreams a place in your prayers and plans. God-given dreams can help you move into the future He is preparing for you.

Barbara Johnson

Plan ahead—it wasn't raining when Noah built the ark.

Anonymous

All God's plans have the mark of the cross on them, and all His plans have death to self in them.

E. M. Bounds

With God, it's never "Plan B" or "second best." It's always "Plan A." And, if we let Him, He'll make something beautiful of our lives.

Gloria Gaither

If we neglect the Bible, we cannot expect to benefit from the wisdom and direction that result from knowing God's Word.

Vonette Bright

More from God's Word

"For I know the plans I have for you"—[this is] the Lord's declaration— "plans for [your] welfare, not for disaster, to give you a future and a hope."

Jeremiah 29:11 HCSB

We know that all things work together for the good of those who love God: those who are called according to His purpose.

Romans 8:28 HCSB

But as for you, you meant evil against me; but God meant it for good, in order to bring it about as it is this day, to save many people alive.

Genesis 50:20 NKJV

A man's heart plans his way, but the Lord directs his steps.

Proverbs 16:9 NKJV

"For My thoughts are not your thoughts, nor are your ways My ways," says the LORD. "For as the heavens are higher than the earth, so are My ways higher than your ways, and My thoughts than your thoughts."

Isaiah 55:8-9 NKJV

MY THOUGHTS ON THIS LESSON

A PRAYER FOR TODAY

Dear Lord, let my plans be pleasing to You.
Give me the wisdom to plant wisely and to reap a harvest
that honors You and Your Son. Amen

Lesson 19

It Pays to Be Hopeful

Make me hear joy and gladness.

Psalm 51:8 NKJV

THE LESSON

Esther never abandoned hope, and neither should we.

A re you an optimistic, hopeful, enthusiastic Christian? You should be. After all, as a believer, you have every reason to be optimistic about life here on earth and life eternal. As English clergyman William Ralph Inge observed, "No Christian should be a pessimist, for Christianity is a system of radical optimism." Inge's words are most certainly true, but sometimes, you may find yourself pulled down by the inevitable demands and worries of life here on earth. If you find yourself discouraged, exhausted, or both, then it's time to ask yourself this question: what's bothering you, and why?

If you're worried by the inevitable challenges of everyday living, God wants to have a little talk with you. After all, the ultimate battle has already been won on the cross at Calvary. And if your life has been transformed by Christ's sacrifice, then you, as a recipient of God's grace, have every reason to live courageously.

> Hope is faith holding out its hand in the dark.
>
> —
>
> *Barbara Johnson*

Are you willing to trust God's plans for your life? Hopefully, you will trust Him completely. Proverbs 3:5-6 makes it clear: "Trust in the Lord with all your heart, and lean not on your own understanding; in all your ways acknowledge Him, and He shall direct your paths" (NKJV).

A. W. Tozer noted, "Attitude is all-important. Let the soul take a quiet attitude of faith and love toward God, and from there on, the responsibility is God's. He will make good on His commitments." These words should serve as a reminder that even when the challenges of the day seem daunting, God remains steadfast. And, so should you.

So make this promise to yourself and keep it—vow to be a hope-filled Christian. Think optimistically about your life, your profession, your family, your future, and your purpose for living. Trust your hopes, not your fears. Take time to celebrate God's glorious creation. And then, when you've filled your heart with hope and gladness, share your optimism with others. They'll be better for it, and so will you.

SOMETHING TO THINK ABOUT

When you experience tough times (and you will), a positive attitude makes a big difference in the way you tackle your problems.

The Christian lifestyle is not one of legalistic do's and don'ts, but one that is positive, attractive, and joyful.

Vonette Bright

The people whom I have seen succeed best in life have always been cheerful and hopeful people who went about their business with a smile on their faces.

Charles Kingsley

We may run, walk, stumble, drive, or fly, but let us never lose sight of the reason for the journey, or miss a chance to see a rainbow on the way.

Gloria Gaither

Make the least of all that goes and the most of all that comes. Don't regret what is past. Cherish what you have. Look forward to all that is to come. And most important of all, rely moment by moment on Jesus Christ.

Gigi Graham Tchividjian

Christ can put a spring in your step and a thrill in your heart. Optimism and cheerfulness are products of knowing Christ.

Billy Graham

MORE FROM GOD'S WORD

My cup runs over. Surely goodness and mercy shall follow me all the days of my life; and I will dwell in the house of the Lord Forever.

Psalm 23:5-6 NKJV

But if we hope for what we do not see, we eagerly wait for it with patience.

Romans 8:25 HCSB

For God has not given us a spirit of fearfulness, but one of power, love, and sound judgment.

2 Timothy 1:7 HCSB

I am able to do all things through Him who strengthens me.

Philippians 4:13 HCSB

Be of good courage, and He shall strengthen your heart, all you who hope in the Lord.

Psalm 31:24 NKJV

MY THOUGHTS ON THIS LESSON

_____

_____

_____

_____

_____

_____

_____

_____

_____

_____

A PRAYER FOR TODAY

Dear Lord, I will look for the best in other people,
I will expect the best from You, and I will try my best
to do my best—today and every day. Amen

Lesson 20

God Gives Us Talents for a Reason: To Use Them

Esther was the daughter of Abihail, the uncle of Mordecai who had adopted [her] as his own daughter.
When her turn came to go to the king, she did not ask for anything except what Hegai, the king's trusted official in charge of the harem, suggested. Esther won approval in the sight of everyone who saw her.

Esther 2:15

THE LESSON

Esther used her gifts, and we should use ours.

God gave Esther an assortment of gifts including beauty, intelligence, and courage. Esther used those gifts to gain favor with the King and to save her people.

All of us have special gifts from the Creator, and you are no exception. But your talent is no guarantee of success; it must be cultivated and nurtured; otherwise, it will go unused . . . and God's gift to you will be squandered.

God knew precisely what He was doing when He gave you a unique set of talents and opportunities. And now, God wants you to use those talents for the glory of His kingdom. But you live in a world that often encourages you to do otherwise.

> Employ whatever God has entrusted you with, in doing good, all possible good, in every possible kind and degree.
>
> —
>
> *John Wesley*

You inhabit a world that is filled to the brim with countless opportunities to squander your time, your resources, and your talents. So you must be watchful for distractions and temptations that might lead you astray.

Your particular talent is a treasure on temporary loan from God. He intends that your talent enrich the world and enrich your life. If you're sincerely interested in building a better life, build it upon the talents that God (in His infinite wisdom) has given you. Don't try to build a career (or a life) around the talents you wish He had given you.

God has blessed you with unique opportunities to serve Him, and He has given you every tool that you need to do so. Today, accept this challenge: value the talent that God has given you, nourish it, make it grow, and share it with the world. After all, the best way to say "Thank You" for God's gifts is to use them.

SOMETHING TO THINK ABOUT

God has given you a unique array of talents and opportunities. The rest is up to you.

Not everyone possesses boundless energy or a conspicuous talent. We are not equally blessed with great intellect or physical beauty or emotional strength. But we have all been given the same ability to be faithful.

Gigi Graham Tchividjian

The Lord has abundantly blessed me all of my life. I'm not trying to pay Him back for all of His wonderful gifts; I just realize that He gave them to me to give away.

Lisa Whelchel

If you want to reach your potential, you need to add a strong work ethic to your talent.

John Maxwell

You are the only person on earth who can use your ability.

Zig Ziglar

God's love for His children is unconditional, no strings attached. But, God's blessings on our lives do come with a condition— obedience. If we are to receive the fullness of God's blessings, we must obey Him and keep His commandments.

Jim Gallery

MORE FROM GOD'S WORD

Do not neglect the gift that is in you.

1 Timothy 4:14 HCSB

I remind you to keep ablaze the gift of God that is in you.

2 Timothy 1:6 HCSB

According to the grace given to us, we have different gifts: If prophecy, use it according to the standard of faith; if service, in service; if teaching, in teaching; if exhorting, in exhortation; giving, with generosity; leading, with diligence; showing mercy, with cheerfulness.

Romans 12:6-8 HCSB

Every generous act and every perfect gift is from above, coming down from the Father of lights.

James 1:17 HCSB

Based on the gift they have received, everyone should use it to serve others, as good managers of the varied grace of God.

1 Peter 4:10 HCSB

My Thoughts on This Lesson

_____

_____

_____

_____

_____

_____

_____

_____

_____

_____

A Prayer for Today

Father, because of Your promises I can live courageously.
But make me fearful of displeasing You. Let me fear complacency
in doing Your kingdom's work, and make me a faithful steward
of the gifts You have entrusted to me. Amen

Lesson 21

Sometimes, We Cannot Remain Silent

*"If you keep silent at this time, liberation and deliverance
will come to the Jewish people from another place,
but you and your father's house will be destroyed.
Who knows, perhaps you have come to the kingdom
for such a time as this."*

Esther 4:14 HCSB

THE LESSON

When God wants us to speak up, we should speak.

Mordecai reminded Esther that there are times when silence is sin, times when we should testify bravely about the things we've experienced and the things we know. Those of us who are Christians should be willing to talk about the things that Christ has done for us. Our personal testimonies are vitally important, but sometimes, because of shyness or insecurities, we're afraid to share our experiences. And that's unfortunate.

In his second letter to Timothy, Paul shares a message to believers of every generation when he writes, "For God has not given us a spirit of fearfulness" (1:7 HCSB). Paul's meaning is crystal clear: When sharing our testimonies, we must be courageous, forthright, and unashamed.

> God is not saving the world; it is done. Our business is to get men and women to realize it.
>
> —
>
> *Oswald Chambers*

We live in a world that desperately needs the healing message of Christ Jesus. Every believer, each in his or her own way, bears responsibility for sharing the Good News of our Savior. And it is important to remember that we bear testimony through both words and actions.

Billy Graham observed, "Our faith grows by expression. If we want to keep our faith, we must share it." If you are a follower of Christ, the time to express your belief in Him is now.

You know how Jesus has touched your heart; help Him do the same for others.

SOMETHING TO THINK ABOUT

Have you made the decision to allow Christ to reign over your heart? If so, you have an important story to tell: yours.

There is no thrill quite as wonderful as seeing someone else come to trust Christ because I have been faithful in sharing the story of my own faith.

Vonette Bright

Nothing else you do will ever matter as much as helping people establish an eternal relationship with God!

Rick Warren

How many people have you made homesick for God?

Oswald Chambers

If we can love folks the way they, are we have greater chance of winning them to the kingdom.

Dennis Swanberg

If you are going to live in peace, you need to embrace in faith the reality that "the LORD is in His holy temple." Embrace it and be silent before Him. You don't need to argue. You don't need to defend God. Simply explain Him as the Word of God explains Him. Then it is the skeptic's responsibility to accept or reject the Word of God. The responsibility is his, not yours. It's between him and God. It's a matter of faith.

Kay Arthur

Faith in small things has repercussions that ripple all the way out. In a huge, dark room a little match can light up the place.

Joni Eareckson Tada

The evangelistic harvest is always urgent. The destiny of men and of nations is always being decided. Every generation is strategic. We are not responsible for the past generation, and we cannot bear the full responsibility for the next one, but we do have our generation. God will hold us responsible as to how well we fulfill our responsibilities to this age and take advantage of our opportunities.

Billy Graham

Our commission is quite specific. We are told to be His witness to all nations. For us, as His disciples, to refuse any part of this commission frustrates the love of Jesus Christ, the Son of God.

Catherine Marshall

More from God's Word

But sanctify the Lord God in your hearts, and always be ready to give a defense to everyone who asks you a reason for the hope that is in you.

1 Peter 3:15 HCSB

You are the light of the world. A city that is set on a hill cannot be hidden. Nor do they light a lamp and put it under a basket, but on a lampstand, and it gives light to all who are in the house. Let your light so shine before men, that they may see your good works and glorify your Father in heaven.

Matthew 5:14–16 NKJV

Whatever I tell you in the dark, speak in the light; and what you hear in the ear, preach on the housetops.

Matthew 10:27 NKJV

And I say to you, anyone who acknowledges Me before men, the Son of Man will also acknowledge him before the angels of God; but whoever denies Me before men will be denied before the angels of God.

Luke 12:8-9 HCSB

My Thoughts on This Lesson

_____

_____

_____

_____

_____

_____

_____

_____

_____

_____

A Prayer for Today

Lord, the life that I live and the words that I speak will tell
the world how I feel about You. Today and every day,
let my testimony be worthy of You. Let my words be sure and
true, and let my actions point others to You. Amen

Lesson 22

God Calls Godly Men and Women to Follow Him and to Lead Others

Shepherd the flock of God which is among you, serving as overseers, not by compulsion but willingly, not for dishonest gain but eagerly.

1 Peter 5:2 NKJV

THE LESSON

Esther was willing to be a courageous leader. When the situation merits, we, too, should be willing to lead.

Some people seem to be born leaders. Others, like Esther, have leadership thrust upon them. We all should prepare ourselves to take on roles God places before us.

John Maxwell writes, "Great leaders understand that the right attitude will set the right atmosphere, which enables the right response from others." If you are in a position of leadership, whether as a parent, or at work, or at church, or at school—it's up to you to set the right tone by maintaining the right attitude.

> Integrity and maturity are two character traits vital to the heart of a leader.
>
> —
>
> *Charles Stanley*

What's your attitude today? Are you fearful, angry, bored, or worried? Are you confused, bitter, or pessimistic? If so, then you should ask yourself if you're the kind of leader whom you would want to follow. If the answer to that question is no, then it's time to improve your leadership skills.

Our world needs Christian leadership, and so do your family members and coworkers. You can become a trusted, competent, thoughtful leader if you learn to maintain the right attitude: one that is realistic, optimistic, forward looking, and Christ-centered.

SOMETHING TO THINK ABOUT

Leadership comes in many forms, and you can lead others in your own way using your own style.

You can never separate a leader's actions from his character.

John Maxwell

A man ought to live so that everybody knows he is a Christian, and most of all, his family ought to know.

D. L. Moody

A wise leader chooses a variety of gifted individuals. He complements his strengths.

Charles Stanley

Leaders must learn how to wait. Often their followers don't always see as far as they see or have the faith that they have.

Warren Wiersbe

What do we Christians chiefly value in our leaders? The answer seems to be not their holiness, but their gifts and skills and resources. The thought that only holy people are likely to be spiritually useful does not loom large in our minds.

J. I. Packer

A true and safe leader is likely to be one who has not desire to lead, but is forced into a position of leadership by inward pressure of the Holy Spirit and the press of external situation.

A. W. Tozer

Don't worry about what you do not understand. Worry about what you do understand in the Bible but do not live by.

Corrie ten Boom

More depends on my walk than my talk.

D. L. Moody

When you discover the Christian way, you discover your own way as a person.

E. Stanley Jones

MORE FROM GOD'S WORD

According to the grace given to us, we have different gifts: If prophecy, use it according to the standard of faith; if service, in service; if teaching, in teaching; if exhorting, in exhortation; giving, with generosity; leading, with diligence; showing mercy, with cheerfulness.

Romans 12:6-8 HCSB

And we exhort you, brothers: warn those who are lazy, comfort the discouraged, help the weak, be patient with everyone.

1 Thessalonians 5:14 HCSB

An overseer, therefore, must be above reproach, the husband of one wife, self-controlled, sensible, respectable, hospitable, an able teacher, not addicted to wine, not a bully but gentle, not quarrelsome, not greedy.

1 Timothy 3:2-3 HCSB

His master said to him, "Well done, good and faithful slave! You were faithful over a few things; I will put you in charge of many things. Enter your master's joy!"

Matthew 25:21 HCSB

My Thoughts on This Lesson

_____

_____

_____

_____

_____

_____

_____

_____

_____

_____

A Prayer for Today

Heavenly Father, when I find myself in a position of leadership,
let me follow Your teachings and obey Your commandments.
Make me a person of integrity and wisdom, Lord, and make me
a worthy example to those whom I serve. And, let me turn
to You, Lord, for guidance and for strength in all
that I say and do. Amen

Lesson 23

When God Is with Us, We Can Be Confident

She said, "If it pleases the king, and I have found approval
before him, if the matter seems right to the king and
I am pleasing in his sight, let a royal edict be written.
Let it revoke the documents the scheming Haman son of
Hammedatha the Agagite, wrote to destroy the Jews who
in all the king's provinces. For how could I bear
to see the evil that would come on my people?
How could I bear to see the destruction of my relatives?"

Esther 8:5-6 HCSB

THE LESSON

Because she knew she was doing God's will, Esther was confident. When we're following God's path, we, too, should be confident.

Esther had confidence in God and confidence in herself. And if you pause to think about it, you'll agree that self-confidence is, at its core, confidence in the Creator. When we put our faith and confidence in our Lord, we enjoy a sense of self-worth and self-confidence. It is something of a paradox that when we are wholly humble and bowed before God, we can then stand tall among our peers with strength and power.

Do you kneel down before God and stand up tall among your peers? And do you place a high value on your time and your talents? Hopefully so. After all, you are created by God, with an array of unique gifts and opportunities, all of which He wants you to use. But if you've acquired the unfortunate habit of devaluing your efforts or yourself, it's now time to revolutionize the way that you think about your career, your capabilities, your opportunities, your future, and your Father in heaven.

> What I believe about God is the most important thing about me.
>
> —
>
> A. W. Tozer

Nobody can build up your self-confidence if you're unwilling to believe in yourself. And the world won't give you very much respect until you decide to respect yourself first. So if you've been talking yourself down or selling yourself short, stop. Remember: If you want to enjoy real abundance—and if you want to be comfortable in your own skin—you need a healthy dose of self-respect . . . a dose that nobody can administer but you and your Creator.

SOMETHING TO THINK ABOUT

Increase your confidence by living in God's will for your life. And remember: The more you trust God, the more confident you will become.

You are valuable just because you exist. Not because of what you do or what you have done, but simply because you are.

Max Lucado

If you ever put a price tag on yourself, it would have to read "Jesus" because that is what God paid to save you.

Josh McDowell

Find satisfaction in him who made you, and only then find satisfaction in yourself as part of his creation.

St. Augustine

Life is a glorious opportunity.

Billy Graham

Give yourself a gift today: be present with yourself. God is. Enjoy your own personality. God does.

Barbara Johnson

Confidence in the natural world is self-reliance; in the spiritual world, it is God-reliance.

Oswald Chambers

Being loved by Him whose opinion matters most gives us the security to risk loving, too—even loving ourselves.

Gloria Gaither

A healthy self-identity is seeing yourself as God sees you—no more and no less.

Josh McDowell

We must understand that the first and chief thing—for everyone who would do the work of Jesus—is to believe, and in doing so, to become linked to Him, the Almighty One, and then to pray the prayer of faith in His Name.

Andrew Murray

MORE FROM GOD'S WORD

For You have made him a little lower than the angels, and You have crowned him with glory and honor.

Psalm 8:5 NKJV

How happy are those whose way is blameless, who live according to the law of the Lord! Happy are those who keep His decrees and seek Him with all their heart.

Psalm 119:1-2 HCSB

Happy is the one whose help is the God of Jacob, whose hope is in the Lord his God.

Psalm 146:5 HCSB

If God is for us, who is against us?

Romans 8:31 HCSB

Finally, brethren, whatever things are true, whatever things are noble, whatever things are just, whatever things are pure, whatever things are lovely, whatever things are of good report, if there is any virtue and if there is anything praiseworthy—meditate on these things.

Philippians 4:8 NKJV

My Thoughts on This Lesson

_____

_____

_____

_____

_____

_____

_____

_____

_____

_____

A Prayer for Today

Dear Lord, You only made one me, and I know that
You love me very, very much. I thank You for Your love, Lord,
and I thank You for the gift of Your Son Jesus. Amen

Lesson 24

Focus on
the Possibilities

Make your own attitude that of Christ Jesus.
Philippians 2:5 HCSB

THE LESSON

Esther focused on the opportunities in front of her, not on the dangers that surrounded her. We, too, should focus on possibilities.

When the world seems darkest, the opportunities for believers are brightest. The tiniest light seems brightest in a darkened room. The dire circumstances Esther faced only accentuated the great opportunity she had to do great things for God and for her people. Esther maintained a can-do attitude, and so should we.

Of course you've heard the saying, "Life is what you make it." And although that statement may seem very trite, it's also very true. You can choose a life filled to the brim with frustration and fear, or you can choose a life of abundance and peace. That choice is up to you—and only you—and it depends, to a surprising extent, upon your attitude.

What's your attitude today? Are you fearful, angry, bored, or worried? Are you pessimistic, perplexed, pained, and perturbed? Are you moping around with a frown on your face that's almost as big as the one in your heart? If so, God wants to have a little talk with you.

God created you in His own image, and He wants you to experience joy, contentment, peace, and abundance. But, God will not force you to experience these things; you must claim them for yourself.

God has given you free will, including the ability to influence the direction and the tone of your thoughts. And, here's how God wants you to direct those thoughts:

Finally brothers, whatever is true, whatever is honorable, whatever is just, whatever is pure, whatever is lovely, whatever is commendable—if there is any moral excellence and if there is any praise—dwell on these things (Philippians 4:8 HCSB).

The quality of your attitude will help determine the quality of your life, so you must guard your thoughts accordingly. If you make up your mind to approach life with a healthy mixture of realism and optimism, you'll be rewarded. But, if you allow yourself to fall into the unfortunate habit of negative thinking, you will doom yourself to unhappiness, or mediocrity, or worse.

So, the next time you find yourself dwelling upon the negative aspects of your life, refocus your attention on things positive. The next time you find yourself falling prey to the blight of pessimism, stop yourself and turn your thoughts around. The next time you're tempted to waste valuable time gossiping or complaining, resist those temptations with all your might.

And remember: You'll never whine your way to the top . . . so don't waste your breath.

SOMETHING TO THINK ABOUT

A positive attitude leads to positive results; a negative attitude leads elsewhere.

I could go through this day oblivious to the miracles all around me, or I could tune in and "enjoy."

Gloria Gaither

The things we think are the things that feed our souls. If we think on pure and lovely things, we shall grow pure and lovely like them; and the converse is equally true.

Hannah Whitall Smith

It's your choice: you can either count your blessings or recount your disappointments.

Jim Gallery

The Reference Point for the Christian is the Bible. All values, judgments, and attitudes must be gauged in relationship to this Reference Point.

Ruth Bell Graham

Attitude is the mind's paintbrush; it can color any situation.

Barbara Johnson

Life is 10% what happens to you and 90% how you respond to it.

Charles Swindoll

MORE FROM GOD'S WORD

Set your minds on what is above, not on what is on the earth.

Colossians 3:2 HCSB

Let this mind be in you which was also in Christ Jesus, who, being in the form of God, did not consider it robbery to be equal with God, but made Himself of no reputation, taking the form of a bondservant, and coming in the likeness of men. And being found in appearance as a man, He humbled Himself and became obedient to the point of death, even the death of the cross.

Philippians 2:5-8 NKJV

But as it is written: "Eye has not seen, nor ear heard, nor have entered into the heart of man the things which God has prepared for those who love Him."

1 Corinthians 2:9 NKJV

For the word of God is living and powerful, and sharper than any two-edged sword, piercing even to the division of soul and spirit, and of joints and marrow, and is a discerner of the thoughts and intents of the heart.

Hebrews 4:12 NKJV

My Thoughts on This Lesson

_____

_____

_____

_____

_____

_____

_____

_____

_____

A Prayer for Today

Dear Lord, help me have an attitude that is pleasing
to You as I count my blessings today, tomorrow,
and every day. Amen

The Suffering Woman

When Christ encountered a woman who had suffered for a dozen years, He healed her in an instant:

And suddenly, a woman who had a flow of blood for twelve years came from behind and touched the hem of His garment. For she said to herself, "If only I may touch His garment, I shall be made well."

But Jesus turned around, and when He saw her He said, "Be of good cheer, daughter; your faith has made you well." And the woman was made well from that hour.

Matthew 9:20-22 NKJV

Just as Christ healed the woman who touched His garment, so, too, can He make us whole if we trust Him completely and give our lives to Him.

Lesson 25

Faith Will Make You Whole

Daughter, be of good comfort;
thy faith hath made thee whole.

Matthew 9:22 KJV

THE LESSON

The quality of your faith will help determine the quality of your day and the quality of your life.

When a suffering woman sought healing by merely touching the hem of His cloak, Jesus replied, "Daughter, be of good comfort; thy faith hath made thee whole" (Matthew 9:22 KJV). Christ's message is clear: we should live by faith. But, when we face adversity, illness, or heartbreak, living by faith can be difficult indeed. Yet this much is certain: whatever our circumstances, we must continue to plant the seeds of faith in our hearts, trusting that in time God will bring forth a bountiful harvest.

Have you, on occasion, felt your faith in God slipping away? If so, consider yourself a member of a very large club. We human beings are subject to an assortment of negative emotions such as fear, worry, anxiety, and doubt. When we fall short of perfect faith, God understands us and forgives us. And God stands ready to strengthen us if we turn our doubts and fears over to Him.

As you enter into the next phase of your life, you'll face many experiences: some good, and some not so good. When the sun is shining and all is well, it is easier to have faith. But, when life takes an unexpected turn for the worse, as it will from time to time, your faith will be tested. In times of trouble and doubt, God remains faithful to you. Do the same for Him.

Are you tapped in to the power of faith? Hopefully so. The hours that you invest in Bible study, prayer, meditation, and worship should be times of enrichment and celebration. And, if your faith is being tested to the point of breaking, know that your Savior is near. Reach out to Him, and let Him heal your broken spirit. Be content to touch even the smallest fragment of the Master's garment, and He will make you whole.

SOMETHING TO THINK ABOUT

You cannot see the future, but God can . . . and you must have faith in His eternal plan for you.

Faith is seeing light with the eyes of your heart, when the eyes of your body see only darkness.

Barbara Johnson

The popular idea of faith is of a certain obstinate optimism: the hope, tenaciously held in the face of trouble, that the universe is fundamentally friendly and things may get better.

J. I. Packer

Just as our faith strengthens our prayer life, so do our prayers deepen our faith. Let us pray often, starting today, for a deeper, more powerful faith.

Shirley Dobson

I am truly grateful that faith enables me to move past the question of "Why?"

Zig Ziglar

MORE FROM GOD'S WORD

Now faith is the reality of what is hoped for, the proof of what is not seen.

Hebrews 11:1 HCSB

Now without faith it is impossible to please God, for the one who draws near to Him must believe that He exists and rewards those who seek Him.

Hebrews 11:6 HCSB

For we walk by faith, not by sight.

2 Corinthians 5:7 HCSB

If you do not stand firm in your faith, then you will not stand at all.

Isaiah 7:9 HCSB

Jesus said, "Because you have seen Me, you have believed. Blessed are those who believe without seeing."

John 20:29 HCSB

MY THOUGHTS ON THIS LESSON

_____

_____

_____

_____

_____

_____

_____

_____

_____

A PRAYER FOR TODAY

Lord, sometimes this world is a terrifying place.
When I am filled with uncertainty and doubt, give me faith.
In life's dark moments, help me remember that You are always
near and that You can overcome any challenge.
Today, Lord, and forever, I will place my trust in You. Amen

Mary and Martha

Mary and Martha were sisters of Lazarus and followers of Jesus, the Savior who raised their brother from the dead. When Jesus came to their home, Martha was concerned with hospitality while Mary was concerned with Christ.

The story of Mary and Martha reminds us that we should never allow ourselves to become so busy that we fail to spend precious moments in the presence of our Lord.

Now it happened as they went that He entered a certain village; and a certain woman named Martha welcomed Him into her house. And she had a sister called Mary, who also sat at Jesus' feet and heard His word. But Martha was distracted with much serving, and she approached Him and said, "Lord, do You not care that my sister has left me to serve alone? Therefore tell her to help me."

And Jesus answered and said to her, "Martha, Martha, you are worried and troubled about many things. But one thing is needed, and Mary has chosen that good part, which will not be taken away from her."

Luke 10:38-42 NKJV

Lesson 26

Christ Is Always with Us, and He Understands Our Pain

Then, when Mary came where Jesus was, and saw Him, she fell down at His feet, saying to Him, "Lord, if You had been here, my brother would not have died." Therefore, when Jesus saw her weeping, and the Jews who came with her weeping, He groaned in the spirit and was troubled. And He said, "Where have you laid him?" They said to Him, "Lord, come and see." Jesus wept. Then the Jews said, "See how He loved him!"

John 11:32-35 NKJV

THE LESSON

God is always near. When you grieve, He remains steadfast . . . and He can comfort you.

When Jesus was told of the news that Lazarus, the brother of Martha and Mary, had died, Christ was overcome with grief, and He wept. But that's not all Jesus did; He also went to the tomb of Lazarus and raised him from the dead.

Jesus' response to the death of Lazarus gives us insight into the heart of God: God's heart is a lamenting heart. When we suffer, God suffers with us. When we grieve, God understands our sadness. When we are worried and anxious, God knows our concerns, and He stands ready to comfort us whenever we sincerely turn to Him.

God's heart is a caring heart, but it is also a marvelously lamenting heart. When we are troubled to the very core of our souls, God feels our suffering, and He laments. Then, in His own perfect time and in His own perfect way, He will heal our pain if we invite Him to rule over our hearts, our lives, and our souls.

SOMETHING TO THINK ABOUT

If you're here, God is here. If you're there, God is there, too. You can't get away from Him or His love . . . thank goodness!

We need never shout across the spaces to an absent God. He is nearer than our own soul, closer than our most secret thoughts.

A. W. Tozer

The Lord Jesus by His Holy Spirit is with me, and the knowledge of His presence dispels the darkness and allays any fears.

Bill Bright

The world, space, and all visible components reverberate with God's Presence and demonstrate His Mighty Power.

Franklin Graham

Let this be your chief object in prayer: to realize the presence of your heavenly Father. Let your watchword be: Alone with God.

Andrew Murray

If you want to hear God's voice clearly and you are uncertain, then remain in His presence until He changes that uncertainty. Often, much can happen during this waiting for the Lord. Sometimes, he changes pride into humility, doubt into faith and peace.

Corrie ten Boom

A sense of deity is inscribed on every heart.

John Calvin

More from God's Word

Draw near to God, and He will draw near to you.

James 4:8 HCSB

You will seek Me and find Me when you search for Me with all your heart.

Jeremiah 29:13 HCSB

Surely goodness and mercy shall follow me all the days of my life: and I will dwell in the house of the Lord for ever.

Psalm 23:6 KJV

I am not alone, because the Father is with Me.

John 16:32 HCSB

But from there, you will search for the Lord your God, and you will find [Him] when you seek Him with all your heart and all your soul.

Deuteronomy 4:29 HCSB

My Thoughts on This Lesson

_____

_____

_____

_____

_____

_____

_____

_____

_____

_____

A Prayer for Today

Heavenly Father, even when it seems to me that You are
far away, You never leave my side. Today and every day,
I will strive to feel Your presence, and I will strive to sense
Your love for me. Amen

Lesson 27

Always Put God First

But the Lord said to her, "My dear Martha, you are worried and upset over all these details! There is only one thing worth being concerned about. Mary has discovered it, and it will not be taken away from her."

Luke 10:41-42 NLT

THE LESSON

You must guard your heart by putting God in His rightful place—first place.

Martha and Mary were sisters who both loved Jesus, but they showed their love in different ways. Mary sat at the Master's feet, taking in every word. Martha, meanwhile, busied herself with preparations for the meal to come. When Martha asked Jesus if He was concerned about Mary's failure to help, Jesus replied, "Mary has chosen better" (Luke 10:42 NIV). The implication is clear: as believers, we must spend time with Jesus before we spend time for Him. But, once we have placed Christ where He belongs—at the center of our hearts—we must go about the business of serving the One who has saved us.

> Love has its source in God, for love is the very essence of His being.
>
> —
>
> *Kay Arthur*

How can we serve Christ? By sharing His message, His mercy, and His love with those who cross our paths. Everywhere we look, it seems, the needs are great and so are the temptations. Still, our challenge is clear: we must love God, obey His commandments, trust His Son, and serve His children. When we do, we claim spiritual treasures that will endure forever.

Does God rule your heart? Make certain that the honest answer to this question is a resounding yes. In the life of every righteous believer, God comes first. And that's precisely the place that He deserves in your heart, too.

Something to Think about

God deserves first place in your life . . . and you deserve the experience of putting Him there.

It is when we come to the Lord in our nothingness, our powerlessness and our helplessness that He then enables us to love in a way which, without Him, would be absolutely impossible.

Elisabeth Elliot

When all else is gone, God is still left. Nothing changes Him.

Hannah Whitall Smith

You must never sacrifice your relationship with God for the sake of a relationship with another person.

Charles Stanley

Choose the opposition of the whole world rather than offend Jesus.

Thomas à Kempis

If we are ever going to be or do anything for our Lord, now is the time.

Vance Havner

A life of intimacy with God is characterized by joy.

Oswald Chambers

If God has the power to create and sustain the universe, He is more than able to sustain your marriage and your ministry, your faith and your finances, your hope and your health.

Anne Graham Lotz

Give God what's right—not what's left!

Anonymous

If God is diligent, surely we ought to be diligent in doing our duty to Him. Think how patient and diligent God has been to us!

Oswald Chambers

MORE FROM GOD'S WORD

And I pray this: that your love will keep on growing in knowledge and every kind of discernment, so that you can determine what really matters and can be pure and blameless in the day of Christ.

Philippians 1:9 HCSB

But seek first the kingdom of God and His righteousness, and all these things shall be added to you.

Matthew 6:33 NKJV

He said to them all, "If anyone desires to come after Me, let him deny himself, and take up his cross daily, and follow Me. For whoever desires to save his life will lose it, but whoever loses his life for My sake will save it."

Luke 9:23-24 NKJV

Let us lay aside every weight and the sin that so easily ensnares us, and run with endurance the race that lies before us, keeping our eyes on Jesus, the source and perfecter of our faith.

Hebrews 12:1-2 HCSB

Do not have other gods besides Me.

Exodus 20:3 HCSB

My Thoughts on This Lesson

_____

_____

_____

_____

_____

_____

_____

_____

_____

A Prayer for Today

Dear Lord, Your love is eternal and Your laws are everlasting.
When I obey Your commandments, I am blessed.
Today, I invite You to reign over every corner of my heart.
I will have faith in You, Father. I will sense Your presence;
I will accept Your love; I will trust Your will; and I will praise You
for the Savior of my life: Your Son Jesus. Amen

The Woman Caught in Adultery

When a woman was caught in adultery, a crowd was prepared to stone her. But, Jesus intervened, as is described in this familiar passage:

But Jesus went to the Mount of Olives.

Now early in the morning He came again into the temple, and all the people came to Him; and He sat down and taught them.

Then the scribes and Pharisees brought to Him a woman caught in adultery. And when they had set her in the midst, they said to Him, "Teacher, this woman was caught in adultery, in the very act. Now Moses, in the law, commanded us that such should be stoned. But what do You say?" This they said, testing Him, that they might have something of which to accuse Him. But Jesus stooped down and wrote on the ground with His finger, as though He did not hear.

So when they continued asking Him, He raised Himself up and said to them, "He who is without sin among you, let him throw a stone at her first." And again He stooped down and wrote on the ground. Then those who heard it, being convicted by their conscience, went out one by one, beginning with the oldest even to the last.

And Jesus was left alone, and the woman standing in the midst. When Jesus had raised Himself up and saw no one but the woman, He said to her, "Woman, where are those accusers of yours? Has no one condemned you?"

She said, "No one, Lord."

And Jesus said to her, "Neither do I condemn you; go and sin no more."

John 8:1-11 NKJV

Lesson 28

Christ Teaches Us to Forgive, Not to Judge

And Jesus said to her,
"Neither do I condemn you; go and sin no more."
John 8:11 NKJV

THE LESSON

God has the wisdom to judge other people, and you don't. So don't be too quick to judge.

Even the most devoted Christians may fall prey to a powerful yet subtle temptation: the temptation to judge others. But as believers, we are commanded to refrain from such behavior. The warning of Matthew 7:1 is clear: "Judge not, that ye be not judged" (KJV).

Are you one of those people who finds it easy to judge others? If so, it's time to make radical changes in the way you view the world and the people who inhabit it.

When considering the shortcomings of others, you must remember this: in matters of judgment, God does not need (or want) your help. Why? Because God is perfectly capable of judging the human heart . . . while you are not. This message is made clear by the teachings of Jesus.

> To be a Christian means to forgive the inexcusable, because God has forgiven the inexcusable in you.
>
> —
>
> *C. S. Lewis*

As Jesus came upon a young woman who had been condemned by the Pharisees, He spoke not only to the crowd that was gathered there, but also to all generations, when He warned, "He that is without sin among you, let him first cast a stone at her" (John 8:7 KJV). Christ's message is clear: because we are all sinners, we are commanded to refrain from judging others. Yet the irony is this: it is precisely because we are sinners that we are so quick to judge.

All of us have fallen short of God's laws, and none of us, therefore, are qualified to "cast the first stone." Thankfully, God has forgiven us, and we, too, must forgive others. Let us refrain, then, from judging our family members, our friends, and our loved ones. Instead, let us forgive them and love them in the same way that God has forgiven us.

Something to Think about

If you're setting yourself up to be the judge and jury over other people, watch out! God will judge you in the same way you judge them. So don't be too hard on other people (unless, of course, you want God to be exactly that hard on you).

Being critical of others, including God, is one way we try to avoid facing and judging our own sins.

Warren Wiersbe

Don't judge other people more harshly than you want God to judge you.

Marie T. Freeman

Turn your attention upon yourself and beware of judging the deeds of other men, for in judging others a man labors vainly, often makes mistakes, and easily sins; whereas, in judging and taking stock of himself he does something that is always profitable.

Thomas à Kempis

God expects us to forgive others as He has forgiven us; we are to follow His example by having a forgiving heart.

Vonette Bright

Forgiveness is actually the best revenge because it not only sets us free from the person we forgive, but it frees us to move into all that God has in store for us.

Stormie Omartian

MORE FROM GOD'S WORD

Have mercy on me, O God, according to your unfailing love; according to your great compassion blot out my transgressions. Wash away all my iniquity and cleanse me from my sin.

Psalm 51:1-2 NIV

If you forgive those who sin against you, your heavenly Father will forgive you. But if you refuse to forgive others, your Father will not forgive your sins.

Matthew 6:14-15 NLT

And be ye kind one to another, tenderhearted, forgiving one another, even as God for Christ's sake hath forgiven you.

Ephesians 4:32 KJV

Whenever you stand praying, forgive, if you have anything against anyone, so that your Father in heaven will also forgive you your transgressions.

Mark 11:25 NASB

Praise the Lord, I tell myself, and never forget the good things he does for me. He forgives all my sins and heals all my diseases.

Psalm 103:3 NLT

MY THOUGHTS ON THIS LESSON

_____

_____

_____

_____

_____

_____

_____

_____

_____

A PRAYER FOR TODAY

Dear Lord, sometimes I am quick to judge others.
But, You have commanded me not to judge. Keep me mindful,
Father, that when I judge others, I am living outside of
Your will for my life. You have forgiven me, Lord. Let me forgive
others, let me love them, and let me help them . . .
without judging them. Amen

Lydia

On his second missionary journey, Paul met with a group of women who gathered for prayer at a riverside near Philippi. Among that group was Lydia, a prosperous woman who was "a worshipper of God" (Acts 16:14 NKJV). After encountering Paul and his group of missionaries, Lydia became a Christian, as described in the following passage:

Therefore, sailing from Troas, we ran a straight course to Samo-thrace, and the next day came to Neapolis, and from there to Philippi, which is the foremost city of that part of Macedonia, a colony. And we were staying in that city for some days. And on the Sabbath day we went out of the city to the riverside, where prayer was customarily made; and we sat down and spoke to the women who met there.

Now a certain woman named Lydia heard us. She was a seller of purple from the city of Thyatira, who worshiped God. The Lord opened her heart to heed the things spoken by Paul. And when she and her household were baptized, she begged us, saying, "If you have judged me to be faithful to the Lord, come to my house and stay." So she persuaded us.

Acts 16:11-15 NKJV

Once she was baptized, Lydia invited Paul and Silas to stay at her house, which they did. Later, when Paul "met with the brothers and encouraged them" (v. 40), Lydia's home became the first Christian church in Philippi.

Lydia proved that the prayers and deeds of a single godly woman can change the world—and you, too, have that power. And, the next move is always yours.

Lesson 29

It Pays to Serve

The greatest among you will be your servant.
Whoever exalts himself will be humbled,
and whoever humbles himself will be exalted.
Matthew 23:11-12 HCSB

THE LESSON

Lydia's story teaches us that God wants us to have willing hands and open hearts.

L ydia chose a life of service, and we should learn from her example. Everywhere we look, it seems, the needs are great, and at every turn, or so it seems, so are the temptations. Still, our challenge is clear: we must love God, obey His commandments, trust His Son, and serve His children. When we place the Lord in His rightful place—at the center of our lives—then we claim spiritual treasures that will endure forever.

If you genuinely seek to discover God's unfolding priorities for your life, you must ask yourself this question: "How does God want me to serve others?"

Whatever your path, whatever your calling, you may be certain of this: service to others is an integral part of God's plan for your life. Christ was the ultimate servant, the Savior who gave His life for mankind. As His followers, we, too, must become humble servants.

> If we want to hear God's voice, we must surrender our minds and hearts to Him.
>
> —
>
> *Billy Graham*

Are you willing to become a humble servant for Christ? Are you willing to roll up your sleeves and do your part to make the world a better place, or are you determined to keep all your blessings to yourself? The answer to these questions will determine the quantity and the quality of the service you render to God and to His children.

Today, you may feel the temptation to build yourself up in the eyes of your neighbors. Resist that temptation. Instead, serve your neighbors quietly and without fanfare. Find a need and fill it . . .

humbly. Lend a helping hand and share a word of kindness . . . anonymously, for this is God's way.

As a humble servant, you will glorify yourself not before men, but before God, and that's what God intends. After all, earthly glory is fleeting: here today and all too soon gone. But, heavenly glory endures throughout eternity. So, the choice is yours: Either you can lift yourself up here on earth and be humbled in heaven, or vice versa. Please choose wisely.

SOMETHING TO THINK ABOUT

The direction of your steps and the quality of your life will be determined by the level of your service.

God wants us to serve Him with a willing spirit, one that would choose no other way.

Beth Moore

No life can surpass that of a man who quietly continues to serve God in the place where providence has placed him.

C. H. Spurgeon

A Christian is a perfectly free lord of all, subject to none. A Christian is a perfectly dutiful servant of all, subject to all.

Martin Luther

If doing a good act in public will excite others to do more good, then "Let your Light shine to all." Miss no opportunity to do good.

John Wesley

You can judge how far you have risen in the scale of life by asking one question: How wisely and how deeply do I care? To be Christianized is to be sensitized. Christians are people who care.

E. Stanley Jones

Doing something positive toward another person is a practical approach to feeling good about yourself.

Barbara Johnson

MORE FROM GOD'S WORD

Worship the Lord your God and . . . serve Him only.

Matthew 4:10 HCSB

A person should consider us in this way: as servants of Christ and managers of God's mysteries. In this regard, it is expected of managers that each one be found faithful.

1 Corinthians 4:1-2 HCSB

If they serve Him obediently, they will end their days in prosperity and their years in happiness.

Job 36:11 HCSB

We must do the works of Him who sent Me while it is day. Night is coming when no one can work.

John 9:4 HCSB

Serve the Lord with gladness.

Psalm 100:2 HCSB

My Thoughts on This Lesson

_____

_____

_____

_____

_____

_____

_____

_____

_____

_____

A Prayer for Today

Lord, You have promised me a life of abundance and joy
through Your Son Jesus. Thank You, Lord, for Your blessings,
and guide me according to Your will, so that I might be a worthy
servant in all that I say and do, this day and every day. Amen

Mary Magdalene

W e conclude with an essential lesson from the life of Mary Magdalene, the most prominent woman among Christ's inner circle of followers. Initially, Jesus had healed her of evil spirits and infirmities, as described in the passage below.

Now it came to pass, afterward, that He went through every city and village, preaching and bringing the glad tidings of the kingdom of God. And the twelve were with Him, and certain women who had been healed of evil spirits and infirmities—Mary called Magdalene, out of whom had come seven demons, and Joanna the wife of Chuza, Herod's steward, and Susanna, and many others who provided for Him from their substance.

Luke 8:1-3 NKJV

After being healed, Mary Magdalene never forgot what her Savior had done. She continued to serve Him, to honor Him, and to share His Good News. She became the most prominent women among His followers, and she was the first person to whom He appeared after the resurrection.

Mary Magdalene was made whole by the transforming touch of Jesus. Then, she followed Him faithfully for the rest of her life. And, so must we.

Lesson 30

The Decision to Follow Him

If anyone serves Me, let him follow Me;
and where I am, there My servant will be also.
If anyone serves Me, him My Father will honor.
John 12:26 NKJV

THE LESSON

Mary Magdalene followed Jesus, and so must we.

After Mary Magdalene was healed by Jesus, she chose to follow Him. She even followed Him in death, to the very tomb that could not hold Him.

Jesus walks with you. Are you really walking with Him? And has He made a radical difference in your life—an unmistakable difference in the way you think and the way you behave? Hopefully, you can answer the questions with a resounding yes. After all, Jesus loved you so much that He endured unspeakable humiliation and suffering. And He did it for you.

How will you respond to Christ's sacrifice? Will you take up His cross and follow Him, or will you choose another path? When you place your hopes squarely at the foot of the cross, when you place Jesus squarely at the center of your life, you will become a radical disciple, and that's precisely the kind of disciple Christ wants you to be.

> We have in Jesus Christ a perfect example of how to put God's truth into practice.
>
> —
>
> *Bill Bright*

The old familiar hymn begins, "What a friend we have in Jesus...." No truer words were ever penned. Jesus is the sovereign Friend and ultimate Savior of mankind. Christ showed enduring love for His believers by willingly sacrificing His own life so that we might have eternal life. Now, it is our turn to become His friend.

As citizens of a fast-changing world, we face challenges that sometimes leave us feeling overworked, overcommitted, and overwhelmed. But God has different plans for us. He intends that we slow down long enough to praise Him and to glorify His Son. When we do, He lifts our spirits and enriches our lives.

Today provides yet another glorious opportunity to place yourself in the service of the One from Galilee. May you seek His will, may you trust His Word, and may you walk in His footsteps. When you do, you'll demonstrate that your acquaintance with the Master is not a passing fancy, but is, instead, the cornerstone and the touchstone of your life.

SOMETHING TO THINK ABOUT

Think about your relationship with Jesus: what it is, and what it can be. Then, as you embark upon the next phase of your life's journey, be sure to walk with your Savior every step of the way.

Christ is not valued at all unless He is valued above all.

St. Augustine

A disciple is a follower of Christ. That means you take on His priorities as your own. His agenda becomes your agenda. His mission becomes your mission.

Charles Stanley

Think of this—we may live together with Him here and now, a daily walking with Him who loved us and gave Himself for us.

Elisabeth Elliot

The heaviest end of the cross lies ever on His shoulders. If He bids us carry a burden, He carries it also.

C. H. Spurgeon

Being a Christian is more than just an instantaneous conversion; it is like a daily process whereby you grow to be more and more like Christ.

Billy Graham

When we truly walk with God throughout our day, life slowly starts to fall into place.

Bill Hybels

MORE FROM GOD'S WORD

We encouraged, comforted, and implored each one of you to walk worthy of God, who calls you into His own kingdom and glory.

1 Thessalonians 2:12 HCSB

The one who loves his life will lose it, and the one who hates his life in this world will keep it for eternal life. If anyone serves Me, he must follow Me. Where I am, there My servant also will be. If anyone serves Me, the Father will honor him.

John 12:25-26 HCSB

"Follow Me," Jesus told them, "and I will make you into fishers of men!" Immediately they left their nets and followed Him.

Mark 1:17-18 HCSB

You did not choose Me, but I chose you. I appointed you that you should go out and produce fruit, and that your fruit should remain, so that whatever you ask the Father in My name, He will give you.

John 15:16 HCSB

Then He said to them all, "If anyone wants to come with Me, he must deny himself, take up his cross daily, and follow Me."

Luke 9:23 HCSB

My Thoughts on This Lesson

_____

_____

_____

_____

_____

_____

_____

_____

_____

_____

A Prayer for Today

Heavenly Father, even when it seems to me that You are
far away, You never leave my side. Today and every day,
I will strive to feel Your presence, and I will strive to sense
Your love for me. Amen

He said to him, "You shall love
the Lord your God with
all your heart, with all your soul,
and with all your mind.
This is the greatest and most
important commandment."

—

Matthew 22:37-38 HCSB